To Molly Sutherland
from
Grandpa Sutherland
Christmas 1955.

The Fables of India

Illustrated
by
Randy
Monk

THE

FABLES OF

INDIA

by

JOSEPH GAER

Little, Brown and Company
Boston · Toronto

Published simultaneously in Canada
by Little, Brown & Company (Canada) Limited

PRINTED IN THE UNITED STATES OF AMERICA

Contents

III. THE BOOK OF GOOD COUNSEL
(*The Hitopadesa*)

Contents   ix

IV. THE BOOK OF BUDDHA'S BIRTH-STORIES
(The Jatakas)

x   *Contents*

One

MAN'S FABLES

FABLERS AND FABULISTS

A man who creates fables is called a "fabler"; and he who edits, or revises, or improvises upon them is called a "fabulist." Strangely enough, when the known fablers of the world are put under a magnifying glass, so to speak, most of them turn out to be not fablers at all, but fabulists.

Take the case of Aesop, the most renowned fabler of the Western world. Aesop, we are told by his biographers, was a Greek slave who lived in the sixth century B.C. He is described by some as one of the homeliest of human beings, "flat-nosed, hunchbacked, bladder-lipped, baker-legged."

The life of Aesop has been described by biographers in colorful terms and in great detail. They have related the life of Aesop reverently and solemnly — as if they had been his contemporaries and seen him with their own observant eyes or heard the fabler with their own attentive ears.

Yet, as a matter of undiluted fact, all we know with certainty about this extraordinary fabler is that his name was Aesop, which is "the same with Ethiop," or "the man from Ethiopia." And that about twenty-five hundred years ago a number of folk fables circulated in Greece. Instead of beginning with, "Once upon a time there was a hare and a tortoise . . ." their stories began with, "I will now tell you a

tale by the Ethiop about the hare and the tortoise . . ."
Because all these tales were attributed to an Ethiop, it was
assumed that he was black and a slave. And to make sure that
no one would judge the wine by the bottle, people later described the Ethiop as repulsive and tongue-tied. The rest of
Aesop's life and adventures were reconstructed, many, many
centuries later, upon this gossamer foundation, entirely wo-
ven out of the web of myths about the fabler which had accumulated through the centuries.

Perhaps the most surprising part of the Aesop myth is that
he was not a fabler, after all, but an extraordinary fabulist.
For we know now with certainty that a number of the fables
attributed to Aesop were known many centuries earlier as
part of the folklore of the Egyptians, the Persians and the
Hindus.

There were fablers before Aesop; and there have been distinguished writers of fables since his time. Practically every
nation has put forward the claim to one or more fables. The
Romans had several, with Phaedrus, who lived in the first
century A.D., as the most outstanding of the Latin fablers.
But actually his work is based on the fables attributed to
Aesop.

The French have their La Fontaine, whose precise and
beautiful fables endeared him to his nation and made his
name beloved throughout the civilized world. The French
insist that though all others in this category might be fabulists, their Jean de la Fontaine was a true fabler. La Fontaine
himself, however, in the preface to his *Fables,* published in
1678, wrote: "It is not necessary that I should say whence I

have taken the subjects of these new fables. I shall only say, from a sense of gratitude, that I owe the largest portion of them to Pilpay [Bidpai] the Indian sage."

The English pride in this field was, and still is, the eighteenth-century poet and dramatist John Gay. We remember Gay best as the author of *The Beggar's Opera,* but some lines from his fables have become part of the idiom of the English language.

The Spanish sing the praises of Don Thomás de Iriarte. The Germans read the *Fabeln* as re-created by Gotthold Ephriam Lessing. And the Russians have their Ivan Krylov. So it goes for every nation.

In every generation a writer comes along who is fascinated by the fable, and he devotes himself to it, worrying little whether he will ultimately be called a fabler or a fabulist.

WHAT IS A FABLE?

Among the many forms of literature the fable is one of the oldest. And it is defined by Dr. Samuel Johnson, in writing about the fabulist John Gay, as "a narrative in which beings irrational, and sometimes inanimate, are, for the purpose of moral instruction, feigned to act and speak with human interests and passions."

The conclusion, or moral, of a fable is usually an accepted proverb. And, in this sense, the fable is a narrative demonstrating a proverb. There is reason to believe that the conclusion of the fable, or its proverb, was created first.

In the dim and distant past, at a time when few could read, or even before the written word was known, men tried to

teach their young about "right" and "wrong" in lessons re-
duced to a few words, easy to understand, easy to remember,
easy to repeat. Those were the earliest proverbs. Afterwards
came the fable, which was used to fix in the memory such
proverbs as "Necessity is the mother of invention," "A bird
in hand is worth two in the bush," and other folk sayings.

As in the case of the proverb, so also in the case of the fable
we cannot discover the name of the original author. The
furthest we ever reach is the name of the remembered fabulist. Fables, like proverbs, myths and allegories, are folk
literature — they are folklore.

Many fables, if not most, deal with animals and even inanimate objects. This might indicate that the fable originated
at a time when people were nature worshippers and believed
that all things which grew, multiplied and perished — from
trees to frogs — had souls or spirits. In those early days it was
not difficult for people to imagine that beasts could speak. This
was particularly true in India. It is easy to understand how
people with great literary talent, who believe in reincarnation,
would treat animals in their stories very much like distant relatives. They would not consider it at all strange that animals
should have human emotions and human failings.

Also, it is less dangerous to expose human foibles and weaknesses by attributing them to animals than to people. Just as
the modern cartoonists often draw animals-in-human-situa-
tions (Pogo, Donald Duck, Br'er Rabbit), so the fablers of
India prudently criticized people and institutions through
animal fables, in which the jackal and the ass, the fox and
the crow were prominent.

The Hindus were the earliest and the greatest of the fablers. Long after the fables of India had multiplied, and even
long after the names of the original authors were forgotten,
other nations drew upon the Hindu fables. The Persians and
the Arabs, the Hebrews and the Greeks, and many other
nations adapted the Hindu fables.

Many of these Hindu fables now exist in two hundred
different versions, retold in more than fifty languages — from
Javanese to Icelandic.

THE FABLES OF INDIA

For centuries the fables of India were told orally to instruct the young. They were preserved in the memory of the
people and multiplied in imaginative minds. We are astonished that the Hindus managed to preserve their sacred books
and their fables through many centuries during which the
written word was comprehensible to so few.

In the early days of many Eastern literatures it was common to attribute a new literary creation to a king, a saint or a
scholar. When a fable was told, the narrator believed it would
gain in prestige if attributed to a holy man or a great teacher.

Later, much later, when these fables were recorded in
writing, the entire collection was credited to one man. From
then on diverse authors and editors made new collections of
fables, leaving out those they did not like and adding others.
Since there was no printing in those days and the written
scripts were highly perishable, many of the very early collections were either entirely lost or survived only in fragments.

What we have now are only those versions of the fables of India which have survived the ravages of time. Of these there exist three outstanding collections:

The Panchatantra, or, The Book of Five Headings;
The Hitopadesa, or, The Book of Good Counsel; and
The Jatakas, or, The Book of Buddha's Birth-Stories.

In the following pages a group of beast fables of enduring value have been selected from these three books. In many instances several versions of one story have been combined; and all selections were made on the basis of their interest to us today. In rewriting the stories, characterizations of animals and plants in India were added to give more reality to the background of these fables; and each fable has been re-created as an independent story, though in the original sources most of them are intricately interwoven in a series of stories-within-stories.

Two

THE BOOK OF
FIVE HEADINGS

(The Panchatantra)

THE PANCHATANTRA

In the beginning fables appeared in India for religious instruction. They were used to teach the merits of truth, humility or self-sacrifice.

But as time went by, and centuries passed, many of the fables, particularly those about animals, were created and collected separately, not for religious education, but for the instruction of princes or nobles in the art of statesmanship — to train them in understanding the human weaknesses that cause the downfall of rulers.

This explains the structure of most of the early collections. First a subject is chosen: How to Conduct a War; or, How to Conclude a Peace; or, How to Make Allies; or, How to Win the Loyalty of Subjects. Then a fable is told which illustrates one aspect of the topic. But before the fable ends, one of the characters in the story raises a different point and starts telling a completely new fable with completely new characters, to illustrate the new subject. Toward the end of the second story, a character raises still another point and starts on a completely new fable. This "Chinese nest" of stories, one within another, continues on and on until the end of the book.

The earliest of fable-collectors for the instruction of princes is known to us simply as Bidpai, or Pilpay, which means "the favorite." In one ancient version of fables this favorite is given as Visnu-Sarman, a wise old man who undertook to teach the art of government to the sons of King Anarasakti. What he taught them is contained in The Five Books, better known as The Book of Five Headings.

According to the introduction to another version, called The Fables of Bidpai, the tyrant king Dobschelin one day ordered the philosopher Bidpai brought before him to speak on the duties of a king. And when Bidpai spoke the truth as he saw it, the displeased tyrant condemned Bidpai to life imprisonment.

Some time later the king was plagued by a problem he could not solve and sent for Bidpai to advise him. So wise was Bidpai's counsel that the king elevated him to the highest office in the royal court. And he urged Bidpai to write down his many ideas on government for the benefit of the rulers of the future. Bidpai then wrote twelve books of fables, each book under a different heading.

Many, many years later, after both king and philosopher were dead, a Persian physician came to India in search of medicinal herbs, and he discovered the Fables of Bidpai. But by that time only five of the twelve original books had survived, and these were known, in Sanksrit, as Panchatantra, which means The Five Books. The Persian physician took The Five Books back to Persia and had them translated from the Sanskrit into the language of his people. This book won the hearts of the Persian people, and was soon translated into Arabic, Greek, Chinese, Hebrew and many other languages. One of the best-known translations of this work in the Western world is the German version by Theodor Benfey.

In different versions and under different names, Bidpai's fables continued to grow in popularity. Some scholars are of the opinion that, with the exception of our Bible, the Panchatantra has received the greatest circulation of any book in world literature.

How much of the Panchatantra, as we have it today in English, resembles the original work, we have no way of knowing. Joseph Jacobs, a noted folklorist at the beginning of this century, tells us that he "edited Sir Thomas North's English version of the Italian adaptation of a Spanish translation of a Latin version of a Hebrew translation of an Arabic adaptation of the Pehlevi version of the Indian original Fables of Bidpai." What has happened to the original fables in the course of this long chain of versions is anybody's guess.

The following animal fables selected from the Panchatantra appear here as separate stories; though, of course, in The Book of Five Headings they are interwoven and interlocked with others in the five groupings of tales under five different headings. Also, these fables originally appeared partly in prose, partly in verse, and were generously interwoven with strings of proverbs on the topic under discussion. In this adaptation they are given simply and directly in prose.

GREEDY AND SPEEDY

In the forests of Lahore there lived two friends, a monkey named Greedy, and a rabbit named Speedy.

One day as they chatted by the roadside, along came a man carrying a cluster of bananas and a bundle of sugar cane balanced on the ends of a pole carried across his shoulders.

Said Greedy to Speedy: "If you were to sit quietly in the middle of the road as if you were hurt, the man would put the burden down and try to catch you. As he nears, you can run away. He will surely follow. And as soon as the two of you are out of sight, I will take his bananas and sugar cane and carry them off to a hiding place. Then, when the man is gone, you can return and we shall both have a great feast."

The rabbit followed the monkey's plan, and it turned out just as he had foretold. The man put his pole down and followed the rabbit, trying to catch him. The rabbit lured the man away a great distance, then raced into a hole and disappeared. Meanwhile the monkey carried off the bananas and sugar cane to the top of a banyan tree.

When the disappointed man returned and found his treasure gone, he cursed the rabbit and he cursed himself, and left. A little while later the rabbit returned and began to look high and low for his friend Greedy.

Finally he spied a pile of banana peelings under a tree. And there, on the top branch of the tree, was the monkey finishing the last banana.

"Where is my share?" asked Speedy.

"You were gone so long," replied Greedy, "and my hunger was so great, that I couldn't wait and I ate it all up."

"How could you eat it all in so short a time?" asked the rabbit.

"If you don't believe me, come up here and see for yourself."

Greedy caught Speedy by his long ears and pulled him up to the top of the tree. "Look and see!" laughed Greedy, then scampered away.

The poor rabbit was afraid to move for fear of falling down and breaking his neck. He remained in the treetop for a long time, wondering how he would ever get down safely. Many animals passed under the tree and Speedy appealed to them for help. But they could not or they would not help him. Until finally a very old rhinoceros came by and stopped to scratch his hide against the tree.

"Dear Rhinoceros," the rabbit pleaded. "You are far-famed for your strength and generosity. Please let me jump down on your back so that I may get out of this tree!"

The rhinoceros, being easily flattered, grunted assent. Speedy tumbled out of the tree and landed on the rhinoceros's neck with such force that the old rhino fell over, broke his neck, and died on the spot.

The frightened rabbit ran away and did not stop until he reached the palace of the king. There he hid himself under the golden throne, just before the king, his courtiers and the royal guard appeared. Silken robes swished and golden swords rattled as the king ascended the throne. The rabbit became so excited that he sneezed.

"Who dares sneeze in the presence of the king?" the monarch demanded.

All the men around the throne looked at each other in terrified silence. Then another sneeze came from right under the golden throne. And Speedy was discovered.

"How dare you sneeze under my throne?" demanded the king. And he gave the order to his executioner: "Off with his head!"

Having nothing to lose now, Speedy pleaded bravely: "If Your Majesty would spare my life, I will lead your men to a large rhinoceros whose great horn, ground into powder, makes wonderful medicine."

The king laughed; then all his courtiers laughed; and the royal guard laughed with them.

"How can a rabbit lead us to a rhinoceros?" asked the king.

"If I fail to do this, you lose nothing, except having my head cut off a little later," said Speedy, feeling quite brave.

The king consented. And Speedy led the courtiers to the animal, high as a man and long as a horse, his three-toed feet up in the air, and the single horn on his nose sticking up in the air three feet high. There was the rhinoceros, just as the rabbit had promised it would be, and quite dead.

When the king was told of the find, he pardoned the rabbit and gave him a royal robe and a horse, as a reward for telling the truth. And the rabbit rode away.

Along the road he met his friend Greedy.

"Where did you get that fine robe and horse?" asked Greedy in surprise.

"The king gave them to me," said the rabbit.

"And why did the king give you all this?"

"Because I sneezed under his throne," answered Speedy.

The monkey did not stop to ask any more questions. "If a foolish rabbit can get so much from the king," thought Greedy, "what will he give to me?" He ran as fast as he could to the royal palace and hid under the golden throne.

Soon the king with his courtiers and the royal guard arrived. Silken robes swished and golden swords rattled as the king ascended the throne. Then the monkey sneezed as loud as he could.

"Who dares sneeze in the presence of the king?" the monarch demanded.

The monkey under the throne sneezed again and louder than before. At once Greedy was dragged out of his hiding place.

"How dare you sneeze under my throne?" demanded the king.

"I did it for a royal robe and a fine steed," said Greedy.

"Indeed!" thundered the king. And he gave the order to the executioner: "Take him away, and off with his head!"

THE FEAST FOR THE FOX

A great hound once hunted a fox, but he could never succeed in catching him. At last, after many a long run, the hound decided that the fox was too sly to be caught in an open chase. So he schemed to trap him with cunning.

He went to the fox's cave, and dug a very deep hole at the entrance. He covered the pit neatly with straw and twigs. And upon them he laid out a tempting meal of birds' eggs and wild grapes carefully placed around a young partridge he had killed that morning.

Then the hound ran off and hid himself near enough to hear what would happen.

The fox returned to his home and saw the feast awaiting him at the door. He sat down and perked up his ears for any sounds. Then he looked at the good food with cunning eyes, and thought:

"It was certainly not there when I left this place. Now, who could have put it there? If a friend wanted to give me all this, he would have brought the gift to me when I was at home. Therefore this must have been brought to me by an enemy for an evil purpose. It is not safe for me to eat it. It is not even safe for me to remain here much longer."

Though he was very hungry and strongly tempted to taste the wonderful food, the fox softly ran away to find safe lodging for the night.

After the fox had left, a hungry leopard came along who smelt the food before he could even see where it was. He dashed blindly toward it, eager for his meal. But as soon as he stepped upon the twigs and straw, the trap collapsed, and he landed at the bottom of the pit.

The hound heard the commotion and congratulated himself on his success in finally trapping the fox. He leaped out of his hiding place and jumped into the pit, happy his scheme had worked so well.

But when he landed at the bottom of the trap he found before him, not his intended victim the fox, but his mortal

enemy, the fierce leopard. And the hound met the fate he had
intended for the fox.

SPOTLESS THE LION AND TRUSTY THE CARPENTER

In a distant forest there once lived a lion whose name was
Spotless. This lion had two great admirers, a jackal and a crow,
who never left the lion's den. Every day the lion went hunting and brought home his prey. And the jackal and the crow
lived royally upon the lion's leavings. After they had eaten
they repeated each day how much they admired their friend
the lion. And that was what Spotless loved to hear even more
than the sound of his own roar.

Now one day a carpenter, named Trusty, and his wife,
named Lusty, came into the forest to cut trees for wood that
he needed. They came early and worked hard. Trusty wan-

dered off to look for more good trees to cut. When he found a tree which seemed just right, he turned to call to his wife to bring his tools. But there, only a few paces away from him, stood Spotless the Lion.

It was too late for Trusty to start running, for the lion was near enough to pounce upon him; and he knew it would do no good to call for help in that deserted spot. Trusty therefore bowed low and smiled as if he had met a neighbor, and said:

"My dear friend Lion, today my wife has prepared a wonderful dinner, and you must come and eat with us."

"My good fellow," said the lion, "I would eat you right now, but you look all bone and gristle. If your wife has prepared tastier food I certainly would prefer it."

Trusty led Spotless to his wife, and Lusty fed the lion a meal of dainties the like of which he had never eaten before.

"If you promise to be my friend and to protect me in this

forest," said Trusty after the meal, "I would like you to come and eat with us again any time you wish."

Spotless promised. And from that day on he gave up hunting for food altogether, for he was pleased with the delicious food the carpenter's wife prepared for him. Trusty the Carpenter was pleased, too, for he no longer feared anyone in the forest, with Spotless to protect him.

But meanwhile the jackal and the crow went hungry. At last they could bear their hunger no longer, and the crow said to the lion:

"Where do you go every day to hunt?"

"I don't go anywhere to hunt," answered Spotless, licking his whiskers.

"But you don't look hungry," said the jackal.

"I'm not hungry. My friends the carpenter and his plump little wife feed me on things I like better than what I can find in the forest."

"Good!" both the jackal and the crow exclaimed. "Let us go and kill the carpenter and his wife, and then we will all have enough to eat!"

But the lion shook his mane. "I promised that I would protect them, and that is why they feed me."

"In that case," said the crow, "ask the carpenter to invite us, too, and let his wife feed us, also, for we are hungry."

"Yes, indeed!" said the cunning jackal. "Since we are your friends he should feed us too."

So the three of them started out to find the carpenter. But when Trusty saw them coming, he shouted to his wife to hide, and he climbed up to the very top of a huge tree.

The lion came up to the tree and asked in surprise: "My good fellow, why did you climb up a tree when you saw me coming? I am your friend! I am Spotless the Lion!"

Trusty looked down from his perch and replied firmly: "I like you, Spotless, and I trust you. But I don't like the looks of your friends."

And never again did Spotless taste the dainties prepared by the carpenter's wife.

THE RESTLESS PIGEON AND HIS WIFE

There was once a pigeon who lived with his turtledove in the eaves of an old building, in a field near a stream. The dove was happy and content. But her restless husband often complained.

"Must we forever live in this hole and never know what goes on in the great world?" he would say.

"Dearly beloved," cooed the dove, "the eaves shelter us from bad weather; the stream supplies us with water; and we can always find wild grain in the field. Why give up all this for the unknown?"

"Only those who travel can acquire knowledge," her husband replied. "The heavens are beautiful because the heavenly bodies are in motion. How could the eloquence of the writer be known if his pen did not move across the page?"

"But look upon the trees," the dove argued patiently. "They do not move and yet they are beautiful and fruitful."

"If the trees could move from place to place, they would

fear neither the saw nor the wedge," the pigeon countered.

Still the turtledove was not convinced. She refused to leave the place she had known all her life and liked so well.

Finally the restless pigeon said to his wife: "If you will not leave this place, let me go alone. I shall tell you about the great world when I return."

Early next morning the pigeon took leave of his wife. Like a bird escaping from a cage, he flew joyfully toward the mountains. All day long he winged his way over rivers and forests, over meadows and valleys. They appeared to him like paradise on earth. As the sun went down, he settled in the branches of a tree to rest for the night.

That evening a great storm arose. The wind coursed through the treetops; flashes of lightning cleaved the darkness, followed by thunder which shook the valleys like an earthquake and reverberated in the mountains with terrifying echoes. Then a cold rain poured down in sudden torrents and continued for hours.

The drenched pigeon hopped from branch to branch in search of protection, chilled to the bone. He thought regretfully of the warmth and safety of the sheltering eaves, and the loving companionship of his wife.

But as soon as the sun appeared over the horizon the pigeon continued on his way. He had not flown very far when he was noticed by a hungry hawk. The pigeon, trembling with fear, flew as swiftly as he could, but he was aware that the hawk was rapidly gaining upon him. "If ever I escape from this danger," thought the pigeon, "I shall never again do anything against my wife's advice."

Just as the hawk was about to sink his talons into the pigeon, a hungry eagle swooped down with the speed of sound to claim the prey for himself. The hawk argued that he had seen the pigeon first and it belonged to him. The eagle replied that he was king of the birds and had prior rights. As the two quarrelsome birds clashed in a fierce battle, the little pigeon escaped. He found a hole in the ground just large enough for him to creep into, and he hid in it for the rest of the day.

The next morning he first looked out carefully to make certain that neither hawk nor eagle was in sight, then started on his way again. After some time he became very hungry and realized that he had eaten no food since leaving home. He flew toward the ground in search of food, and to his great joy discovered a field with corn scattered on the ground and another pigeon feeding upon it.

He alighted hungrily and started to eat ravenously. But when he tried to move, he found out that his feet were caught in a snare.

"Brother, why did you not warn me of the danger?" he asked the other pigeon.

"You, like myself, should have known that where there is an abundance of food in an unguarded field, there must be also a snare. We are both caught in our own folly."

"How can I get out?" cried the restless pigeon.

"If I knew the answer to that," replied the other, "I would deliver myself. However, I have heard it said that when you are in trouble, rely upon yourself and do not let despair make you weak."

The pigeon heeded the good advice and started at once to peck at the cord that held his feet. Soon he freed himself. He was so happy to be released that he even forgot his hunger and started to fly directly for home.

On the way he paused to rest on a wall near a newly sown field. The farmer saw the pigeon and mistook him for a seed thief. He flung a rock at the bird and the stunned pigeon fell from the wall into a dry well nearby. When the farmer came to look for the bird, he could not find him. And the pigeon, whose wing had been broken, remained in the well all night, unable to stir. A thousand times during that night he blamed himself for not heeding his wife.

The next morning the pigeon's wings were strong enough to lift him out of the well. Slowly he made his way home.

The turtledove joyfully welcomed him. She fluttered about to make him comfortable; and she brought him some food.

The tired pigeon told his wife all the adventures that had befallen him out in the great world. But he assured her that the pleasantest of all the sights he had seen was the sheltering eave of the old building, in the field near the stream.

THE CAMEL AND HIS NEIGHBOR

Long ago two neighbors lived in the south of Madura. And though one was a camel and the other a jackal, they became good friends.

One day the hungry jackal said to the hungry camel: "My friend, I know of a field full of tender sugar cane where you can have a great feast."

"Lead me there," said the camel eagerly.

"I would gladly do that," answered the jackal, "but it is on the other side of the river and, as you know, I cannot swim."

"I will carry you on my back," said the camel. "And while I eat the cane, you can feast on the crabs and fish so abundant on that side of the shore."

The camel, with the jackal on his back, swam across the river. The jackal pointed out the sugar-cane field nearby, and then he began to race up and down the shore, gluttonously cramming his mouth with bits of fish and gulping down the abundant crabs. By the time the camel had reached the sugar cane, the jackal was already sated. And since he could not eat any more, he ran up and down howling his contentment at the top of his voice.

The villagers heard the howls and said to each other: "There is a jackal in our sugar cane, scratching holes in the ground and uprooting our plants."

They came running into the field with cudgels, and to their surprise found no jackal but a camel eating their sugar cane. They beat him unmercifully and the poor camel fled toward the river.

"Let us hurry into the water and get across before the villagers catch up with us," begged the jackal, as he jumped upon the camel's back.

The camel swam with all his might for a while, then he

asked: "Tell me, friend Jackal, why did you howl as soon as you had eaten your fill? You aroused the villagers before I barely had a chance to taste the sugar cane!"

"I really don't know," replied the jackal. "It is a habit of mine. As soon as I am sated, I like to howl."

By this time they had reached the deepest part of the river.

"I think that I shall roll over on my back here," said the camel.

"Oh, no!" shouted the jackal. "Why must you do it now? I can't swim!"

"Sorry," said the camel, "but it is a habit of mine. After I have tasted sugar cane, I must roll."

Whereupon the camel rolled over on his back. The jackal fell off and was drowned. But the camel swam safely home.

THE TWIN PARROTS

A mother parrot lived in the mountains of Amritsar, in the district of Lahore. She was always festive in her green and red and blue plumage; and she was very happy with her growing twins, who were as alike as two seeds in a carob pod. Daily the mother parrot left her nest in the hollow of an old tree to search for food. And after she had returned and fed her young until they were sated, the mother parrot taught her twins all that good little parrots should know. She taught them how to fly and how to climb. She showed them how to crack nuts. She trained them to hold their food with the claws of one foot, while with the other they clasped the branch like a vise. Most of all she taught them how to keep out of sight and out of trouble.

The twins grew fast and learned their lessons well; and the mother parrot delighted in her clever children.

But one unhappy day, when the mother parrot returned to her nest, she found it empty. And though she searched everywhere for her twins, she never saw her children again.

For, while the mother parrot was off in search of food, a wily hunter snared her twins and sold them for a good price. One parrot he sold to a brigand who robbed unwary travelers in a distant forest; and the other he sold to a Brahman who lived in his hermitage in another part of that same forest.

A long time passed — one year, two years, or even three years — and the twins grew up apart, one in the hut of the bandit and the other in the home of the hermit.

A king came riding through that forest one day. He raced ahead of his guard and was soon separated from them. When he stopped to look about him he realized that he was lost. The king tried to find a road or path which would lead him back home, or a dwelling where someone could direct him to the highway. Finally the king reached the hut belonging to the bandit. The parrot saw the king approaching, and began to shout:

"Come quickly, my master! Here is a rider on a horse! Come, bind him and kill him! Come, bind him and kill him! Come, bind him and kill him!"

On hearing these frightening words, the king turned his horse about and sped away. He rode at breakneck speed in the opposite direction, until he came close to the hermitage belonging to the Brahman. And the Brahman's parrot, on seeing the king nearing, began to call out gently:

"O Hermit! A guest is coming! Come, feed him and pay him honor! Come, feed him and pay him honor! Come, feed him and pay him honor!"

The king dismounted and said to the parrot:

"Just a while ago, in another part of this forest I encountered a parrot so much like you that he might have been your twin brother. But whereas you are kind and speak gently, he was vicious and kept shouting: 'Come, bind him and kill him! Come, bind him and kill him!'"

"He might have been my twin brother," replied the parrot. "But I was taught by a saintly Brahman; he must have been taught by a murderous brigand. And that is the difference between us."

THE ADDER AND THE FOX

A caravan camped in a thicket one night and when it left in the morning failed to put out the campfire. The embers smoldered all day long. When evening came a breeze ran through the ashes and fanned the sparks until they started a blaze in a nearby bush in which a brown adder was fast asleep. The snake, wakened by the flames which surrounded him, began to call for help.

At that moment a Brahman came riding by on a camel. He heard the plea of one of God's creatures in distress and called out: "Though I know you to be the enemy of mankind, old Viper, I shall nevertheless try to save you, since the saving of any life is considered a good deed."

The Brahman took a sack, tied it to the end of a long stick and held it out over the flames into the center of the burning bush. The adder quickly jumped into the sack and the Brahman pulled him out to safety.

But as soon as the adder slid out of the sack he raised his flat head, flickered his fangs, and threatened to poison the man and his camel.

"You venomous monster!" cried the Brahman. "Have you no gratitude at all that you repay a good deed with evil?"

"I am dealing with you," replied the adder, "only as you humans deal with others."

"I do not believe that you will find another creature on earth who will agree with you," said the Brahman.

"I am willing to let any other creature judge between us," said the adder. "Let us go together, and the first creature we meet shall decide which one of us is right."

The first creature they met was a cow tethered in a pasture. They approached the cow and asked how she thought men repaid kindness and good deeds.

The cow replied sadly: "I can tell only of my own experience. For years I have supplied my master's house with milk, cheese and butter. Every year I have brought him a calf. But now that I am growing old and cannot produce as much as before, he has put me out here in the pasture to fatten so that he may sell me to the butcher next month."

"Now what do you say, Brahman?" asked the adder triumphantly.

"This cow has a grudge against her master and is therefore not impartial in her judgment. Let us try another."

The adder agreed, and they walked along until they came to a big tree. Then the adder said:

"Here is one of God's creations that has long been the friend of man. Let us ask the tree to judge between us."

They presented their case, and the tree replied:

"I protect men from the heat of the sun; I yield them a crop of fruit each year; I give them the sap for a delicious drink. And what do I get in return? My branches are cut down for walking sticks, or handles for my enemy, the hatchet. When I grow old, my trunk will be cut down for planks to walk upon. That is how man repays me for my good deeds!"

"What do you say now, Brahman?" exulted the adder.

"The tree is not a good judge of good or of evil," said the Brahman in confusion. "Let us ask just one more creature, then I will abide by the decision, whatever it may be."

The adder consented and they went on their way.

Soon they met a fox, and the Brahman explained: "I saved this adder's life, and now he threatens to poison me and my camel."

"Explain to me, first, how you rescued this adder," said the fox, as soberly as a judge.

The Brahman explained that he had tied the little sack to a stick and the adder had leaped into it.

The fox began to laugh. "You want me to believe that so

large an adder climbed into so small a sack? That is quite impossible!"

Both the adder and the Brahman tried to assure the fox that it was not only not impossible, but exactly what did happen.

"I cannot believe it," insisted the fox, "unless you prove to me that the adder can really get into that small sack."

"That is very easy to prove," said the adder.

And as the Brahman held out the stick with the sack on its end, the adder slithered into it.

"Good," said the fox to the Brahman. "Now tie the sack and deal with the ungrateful monster as he deserves."

THE CROW IN THE BANYAN TREE

In a forest near Benares, there once grew a banyan tree that was a giant even among giant banyans. It rose over a hundred feet in height, and its spreading trunks and branches covered such an enormous area that it looked more like a large grove of trees than just a single banyan tree. Its bright-green, heart-shaped leaves were a palm's width, and its berries were bigger than cherries.

A crow flew over the tree one day and at once fell in love with it. "Here," thought he, "I shall build my nest, find a wife, and raise a family. And I shall live in this beautiful tree all the days of my life."

Without a moment's delay he started to build his nest in the crook of a very high branch. With much effort and great care he built a nest worthy of his pride, and into it he brought his bride, and there they started to raise a family.

But, alas, in the hollow of the trunk of that beautiful tree there dwelt an ugly black snake. As soon as the little crows were hatched, the snake made its way silently and undetected to the top of the tree; and when the parents left the nest in search of food for their children, the snake devoured the newly born crows.

The hen-crow cried and lamented when she realized what had happened to her children. She pleaded with her husband to go elsewhere and build another nest. But he was unwilling to leave the lovely banyan tree.

"Let us rather try again to raise a family, and hope that no evil will befall us," he argued.

They tried again. And again the black snake came up from the hollow of the trunk and devoured their young.

The hen-crow begged her husband in despair: "Let us move away! For, as long as we stay here, that terrible snake in the trunk of this tree will be our deadly enemy, and I cannot bear the grief of once more losing my children."

Her husband listened patiently. Then he replied: "My grief is as great as yours. But we have lived in this tree very long and it has been good to us. It has given us shade in the heat, and shelter in the rain; and always it has given us plenty of berries to eat. If we go elsewhere we may find, after all the trouble of building a new nest, that another black snake is hidden in the trunk. The best thing would be for us to kill this villain who lives down below us."

"But the snake is deadly poisonous," his wife protested. "How can we possibly kill him?"

"I shall go to my wise friend the fox and ask his advice," replied her husband. "He may be able to contrive some way for us to destroy our enemy."

The crow went to his dear friend the fox and told him about the murderous black snake.

After thinking the matter over carefully, the fox said: "There is a way in which you may destroy your enemy. But you must follow my instructions exactly."

This the crow gladly promised.

Early the next morning the crow flew to the nearest palace, and there he saw the queen and the women of the court bathing in the royal pool. On the grassy bank nearby lay their clothes and jewels. The crow swooped down on the ornaments gleaming in the sun, and picked up in his beak a valuable pearl necklace. Then he flew very slowly in the direction of his banyan tree.

The royal guards, who had seen the bird fly down and carry off a necklace, snatched up clubs and cudgels and ran as fast as they could to keep the thief in sight. As they neared the banyan tree they saw the necklace fall from the beak of the crow and drop into the hollow of the tree.

They hurried to the tree and peered into the hollow. There they saw the stolen necklace, and upon it lay a black, flat-headed snake, which showed its terrible fangs and hissed at the intruders. The king's men clubbed the snake to death, retrieved the priceless necklace and returned to the palace.

And the crow and his wife lived on happily in their nest in the beautiful banyan tree.

THE FALCON AND THE HEN

"Of all the ungrateful creatures on earth," said the falcon to the hen, "you are the most wanting in gratitude."

"Now, what have I done to deserve this from you?" clucked the offended hen.

"Can there be any greater ingratitude than you show your masters? Each day they provide you with food; and each night they give you a roost in shelter and bar the door to any prowlers. Yet, when one of your masters comes near you, you run off as if he were your worst enemy. Now take me, for instance. When a man shows me the least consideration, I stand quietly upon his shoulders, and eat out of his hands."

"What you say is quite true," replied the hen. "But tell me, have you ever seen a falcon upon a spit or in a boiling pot? Of course not. But I have seen many hens boiled, broiled and roasted in a hundred different ways. That is why I don't trust my masters!"

And the hen turned away from the falcon and went on scratching the ground for worms.

THE JACKAL AND THE DRUM

One day a hungry jackal prowled in search of food, but he could find nothing to still his sharp pangs of hunger. He wandered far from his usual hunting grounds, until he blundered onto a battlefield. As he looked about him furtively to figure out how to escape the danger zone, he suddenly heard a terrible sound, like rolling thunder.

The jackal shivered with fear. "The creature that made that sound," he thought, "must be very mighty and swift. If he sees me, he will destroy me with a single blow."

The frightened and dejected jackal dared not move. He remained crouched there, each moment expecting his doom. But nothing happened. After some time the jackal heard the sound again. And again there followed a long silence.

The jackal's curiosity grew greater than his fear. He slowly crept in the direction of the sound he had heard; and he soon came upon a huge, abandoned war drum. As the wind shook down wild nuts from the trees and they chanced to fall upon the drumhead, the drum sent out the terrible rolling thunder. But when no nuts fell upon it, the drum remained silent and peaceful.

The jackal finally approached the drum and slowly circled it several times. After a while he even struck it with his paw. He struck it over and over again, and began to feel very proud, as if he himself were issuing the deafening sounds.

"How lucky am I!" exclaimed the jackal. "After looking for food so long, I have at last found a great treasure. For surely this drum must be full of meat and fat. Otherwise why would anyone want to seal it so tightly on both sides!"

He immediately set to work gnawing at the drumhead. And he nearly broke his sharp teeth before he succeeded in tearing open a hole large enough for him to crawl inside. But once within the drum, the jackal was bitterly disappointed, for he saw it contained only its wooden cylinder.

The jackal left, hungrier than ever, sadly wondering how anything with so fierce a voice could be so completely empty.

THE GARDENER AND THE BEAR

In a deserted valley at the foot of the Himalaya Mountains lived a man who loved gardening more than anything else in the world. He built himself a tiny hut in the very center of his garden and spent all his waking hours working on the plants. He had no wife; he had no children; and he did not keep even a cat or a dog lest they should take some of his time from his work, which was also his greatest pleasure.

After some years of living like this the gardener became lonely. And one day he started out in search of a person or an animal who would live with him and drive his loneliness away.

A short distance along his way he met a huge shaggy bear. This great bear was placid and peaceful, and even eager to be friendly. The gardener greeted him cordially, inquired after his health and asked what he was doing on the road.

The bear replied that he had been living by himself on the top of the mountain and had grown very lonely. At that very moment he was out in search of a companion to live with him.

The gardener was delighted and said: "I, too, am out in search of a companion. I would invite you to come and live with me in my garden, where I have many kinds of fruits and vegetables and plenty of honey — if you would promise never to hug me."

The bear solemnly promised never to hug the gardener, and together the two went to the hut in the beautiful garden. The man spread a great feast before his guest and they each made a vow of eternal friendship.

A deep affection grew up between the man and the bear. The gardener took good care of the bear; and the bear, whenever his friend lay down in the shade of a tree for a nap, stood on guard to protect him and to drive off any insects that might disturb him.

One day the gardener grew weary from work in the heat of the sun. He lay down to rest and was soon fast asleep. And the bear stood by at his post to keep off the flies. Soon he noticed a fly alight on the corner of the sleeping man's mouth. The bear gently waved his paw and drove the fly away. The insect circled in the air and alighted on the other side of the man's mouth. Again the bear drove off the annoying insect. But the fly returned, and this time alighted on the man's nose. The gardener was perspiring; and the fly unfurled its tiny tongue, lapping up the salty droplet as if it were licking a lump of sugar. This tickled the man and he twitched his nose in his sleep.

By this time the bear began to lose his patience. He swiped at the fly with his paw, trying to hit it as it flew into the air. He missed. The insect pest flew around in a wide circle, then came right back, settling on the gardener's forehead.

This impudence filled the bear with anger. He picked up a rock and aimed it at the insufferable fly. His aim was perfect. He killed the fly instantly. But he also crushed the gardener's skull.

THE ELEPHANT AND THE GNAT

In a certain jungle in the south of India a song sparrow and his wife were building their nest in the low branch of a banyan tree. Early and late the sparrows went about their business, always singing a cheery song. And neither rain nor storm could dampen their spirits.

The mother sparrow laid five little eggs in the completed nest, and settled upon them to hatch out a brood of song sparrows.

One day a huge wild elephant stopped to rest in the shade of the banyan tree. He leaned against the trunk to scratch his thick skin and shook the branches like an earthquake. Then he sent his trunk into the tree out of sheer mischief, sniffing and pulling at the twigs and lower branches. The frightened sparrows flew to safety, but their nest crashed to the ground and the eggs in it, almost fully hatched, were trampled under the elephant's feet.

The mother sparrow was beside herself with grief. Nothing her husband could say would comfort her. Then their neighbor, Ivory-Bill the Woodpecker, tried to console her. He said:

"The difference between the wise and the foolish is that the wise know lamenting cannot bring the dead back to life again, but the foolish continue to lament."

"That is true," answered the grief-stricken mother. "But my sorrow would not be so great if I knew of a way to avenge myself on this villainous elephant."

"If revenge will make you feel better," said the woodpecker, "come with me to my friend the singing gnat, who is very wise. Let us ask him how the elephant can be punished."

The gnat listened carefully to the story of the grieving sparrow. Then he said:

"I know how he can be punished. But before that can be done we must get the help of my good friend Rana the Bullfrog."

The sparrow, the woodpecker and the singing gnat went to the pond where Rana lived and told him the reason for their visit. Then the gnat said:

"We must work together. For how can a gnat, or a bullfrog, or even a woodpecker alone hurt the wild elephant? But together we can destroy him."

The sparrow was asked to stand by, while the gnat, the bullfrog and the woodpecker went forth to punish the evil-doer.

First the gnat climbed into the elephant's ear and began to buzz and sing so sweetly that the great animal became drowsy and shut his eyes.

When the elephant fell fast asleep the woodpecker flew up

and pecked out his eyes. The enraged elephant, wakened from his slumber, trumpeted in pain so long and so loud that he became very thirsty.

And then Rana the Bullfrog seated himself at the edge of a very deep pit and started to croak as loud as a bellowing bull.

The elephant followed the sound, certain that where a bullfrog croaked he would find water. But instead he stumbled into the pit, and there the wild elephant perished.

THE BRAHMAN AND THE VILLAIN

Once upon a time there lived in Bangalore a very holy man (called in India a Brahman) whose name was Self-Sacrifice. He was a very good man and devoted all his time to prayer and contemplation. But in the meantime his wife and children were often in dire need.

Daily his wife scolded him, saying: "You are not holy, but lazy. Your heart is made of stone. Instead of sitting about mumbling prayers, why don't you go out and find us some food to eat?"

The Brahman tired of his wife's nagging and one day left his home in search of food. He walked and walked, still contemplating and praying, without realizing that he had wandered off into a dense forest. By that time he had become very hungry and his thirst was even greater than his hunger. He began to look for a brook or spring, and he finally found a well so overgrown with weeds that one could easily fall into it as into a trap.

The Brahman cleared the opening; and when he looked in

to see whether there was any water in it, he saw, far, far down, a tiger, a monkey, a snake and a man who had been trapped in the overgrown well.

The tiger was the first to notice the Brahman peering down into the well, and he called out:

"Holy sir! Please take me out of here! No one knows better than you the merit of saving a life! Please release me from this prison so that I may return to my family, who this very minute must be lamenting my failure to return home."

"Why, Tiger," said the Brahman, "your very name and your voice send shivers down my back! I fear tigers. How then can I save you?"

"Holy and noble sir," said the tiger, "I pledge and promise under the sacred triple oath that neither danger nor harm shall ever come to you because of me!"

"It is better to meet disaster while saving a life," thought the Brahman, "than to suffer from a bad conscience because of lack of pity for a living creature in distress."

And so he pulled the tiger out.

The tiger thanked the holy man and said: "Do you see those mountains yonder? My cave is in a ravine near the highest peak. If ever you come that way, I wish you would visit me so that I may repay you for your kindness this day."

Then the tiger turned and ran off toward the mountains.

Now the monkey began to plead with the Brahman. And the holy man pulled the monkey out of the deep well.

"My home is near the waterfall, not far from the tiger's cave. If ever you come that way, please pay me a visit for I would like to repay you for your kindness this day."

And the monkey leaped onto a branch of a nearby banyan tree and was soon out of sight.

Then the Brahman heard the snake plead: "Please, Brahman, pull me, too, out of this dark and dank prison-well!"

"Really!" said the Brahman. "I can see your color and it is black; I can see your head and it is flat. And it is said that a poisonous snake kills by touching. How can I pull you up out of the well without touching you?"

"O holy man," said the snake, "consider this: I am as the Creator made me. Despise me not, but help me. And I promise you under the sacred triple oath never to harm you!"

The Brahman pulled the black snake out of the well.

"If you are ever in trouble," said the snake, "call for me, and I shall come to your aid." Then the snake slid away and disappeared in the tall grass.

By this time the man in the well was shouting impatiently: "Brahman! Brahman! What about me? You have saved all the vile creatures so far. But I, a human being like yourself, still linger in this dirty well!"

The Brahman, full of contrition, hastened to pull the man out of the well. And the man said:

"I am Somnath the Goldsmith of Bangalore. If you ever have any gold to be worked on or to sell, bring it to me and I shall treat you well, because of the help you have given me this day."

Then Somnath the Goldsmith departed.

The Brahman continued on his journey. He wandered for many days, dejected because he could find nothing of value to take home to his family. Then he recalled the monkey's invitation to visit him.

The Brahman slowly climbed the mountain and after some time found the monkey near the waterfall. The monkey was delighted to see him and gave the Brahman all the sweet fruit he could carry.

"You have proven yourself to be a real friend," said the Brahman, "for I was just on the point of returning to my family empty-handed. Now that I am so near the tiger's home, will you lead me to him, for I want to see whether he remembers me."

The monkey led the Brahman to the tiger's cave. And when the tiger saw them approaching, he came forward, bowed before the holy man so that he touched the ground with both his ears, and said:

"I am happy to see you, honored sir! For I have something to give you in return for your kindness to me."

Thereupon he gave the Brahman a number of gold ornaments studded with precious stones.

"How did you obtain these?" asked the Brahman, afraid to touch them for fear that they had been stolen.

"They were obtained honorably," replied the tiger. "A young prince came into this forest to hunt for tigers. It was his life against mine, and I won. For his arrow missed me and I pounced upon him before he could draw another. From his person I took these ornaments, which are of no use to me. Take them, for I won them fairly in the fight."

The Brahman thanked him for the treasure and went directly to Somnath the Goldsmith.

"I have come into the possession of valuable ornaments that I do not need," said the Brahman. "Sell them for me that I may have money for my wife and children."

Somnath examined the ornaments and at once recognized them as belonging to the young prince who had disappeared during a recent hunting trip.

"Certainly! Certainly!" said Somnath with a friendly smile. "You wait here for me while I show your ornaments to someone who will pay you a fortune for them."

The goldsmith ran directly to the palace and showed the ornaments to the king.

"These jewels belong to my son!" exclaimed the king. "Where did you get them?"

"In my house there is at this very moment a man pretending to be a Brahman, who tried to sell them to me. Surely the villain waylaid your son in the forest, murdered the prince and then robbed him," said Somnath, hoping to receive a reward for the information.

The king dispatched the royal guard to seize the Brahman and have him executed the following day.

While the Brahman lay in his prison cell, his hands and fcct securely tied, he suddenly remembered the snake he had saved and the promise it had made. He wished sadly that in some way the snake could come and break his bonds.

The thought had scarcely entered his head when the snake appeared before him, and said:

"What good will it do you if I break your bonds? You cannot escape from this cell. And if you could, you would be caught again by the king's men and brought back."

"What then can I do?" asked the Brahman, hopelessly.

"I have a plan," said the snake. "I shall bite the queen, who is dearer to the king than the apple of his eye. No matter how they try, they will not be able to save her life. Only the touch of your hand will cure her of my poison. And when you save the queen's life, the king will set you free."

The next day the king was in great distress. He had summoned all his physicians, conjurers and healers to cure the queen, who had been bitten by a poisonous snake, but none of them could help her. In the midst of all the commotion in the palace, word was brought to the king that the Brahman who was to be executed that morning had claimed he could save the queen's life. The king immediately ordered the prisoner brought to the queen's quarters. The Brahman arrived and took the queen's hand as the snake had instructed him. Instantly the queen was restored to health.

The king honored the Brahman and begged forgiveness for having condemned him without a trial. He urged the holy man to tell exactly how he had come into possession of the prince's jewels. And the Brahman related all that had happened to him from the moment he left his home.

The king then ordered the arrest and imprisonment of Somnath the Goldsmith. And he rewarded the Brahman with a thousand villages and the title of viceroy.

The Brahman gathered together his proud wife and children, the numerous relatives on both sides of the family, their many old friends, and they all lived happily ever after in the royal palace.

Three

THE BOOK OF
GOOD COUNSEL
(The Hitopadesa)

THE HITOPADESA

The great collection of fables called the Hitopadesa is considered only an important version of the Panchatantra, but it contains a number of fables not found in other collections. The introduction to this collection begins with the following legend:

The good King Sudarsana lived in the great city of Pataliputra on the banks of the holy Ganges River. One day the king heard a wise man recite:

"Reckless youth, great wealth, high rank, and lack of consideration for others — each, singly, leads to harm; how much more so where the four are combined in the same person!"

The good king thought of his own sons, who were not gaining wisdom, nor studying the sacred books, but following all the improper courses. "As one bright moon gives more light than a host of stars," the king reflected, "so one wise son is better than a thousand fools. And my sons are not fools. They are just uninstructed. The fault is mine."

After reflecting in this manner the king called together his learned advisers and asked them how he could interest his sons in study, which up to that time they had spurned. Thereupon one pandit, Visnu-Sarman by name, arose and said:

"Your sons the princes, O King, come from a great family and have understanding. It is only the method by which they have been taught that is at fault. If I could be allowed six months I would make Your Majesty's sons well versed in the knowledge of government and good conduct."

The king was delighted and turned over his sons for instruction to the learned pandit.

The wise pandit gathered the young princes about him informally on the terrace of the palace, and asked:

"My princes, have you ever heard the story of the crow, the tortoise, the deer and the mouse?"

"No, we have not heard it!" said the princes. "Please, sir, tell it to us!"

"Listen to me carefully," said the pandit, "for I am about to tell you a story about the Acquisition of Friends. And this is how it begins . . ."

And the book of fables is begun.

The purpose of the book is to instruct. But the reason it survived through the centuries was not because it was so educational, but because it was so entertaining. The princes were willing to learn from the old pandit since his ideas were illustrated in such delightful stories, and the rest of the world ever since has been just as eager to listen to them for the same reason.

These fables soon became known and loved throughout India. They were told and retold so often that the stories of The Book of Good Counsel became as familiar to Hindus, young and old, as the family washing.

The fables selected from this book are not found in the Panchatantra, and have been recast to free them from their relation to the story-within-a-story-within-a-story, as given in the original.

However, as an example of the device used in the Hitopadesa to link fable to fable and event to event, one rather long story, "The War of the Cranes and the Peacocks," is given at the end of this section. In the latter part of this story appears the typical device of a story-within-a-story, where the vulture tells the peacock one of the world's most beloved fables, about "The Brahman in the Potter's Shop."

This device has been adopted by writers the world over. It is used in the *Arabian Nights,* or *A Thousand and One Nights* (in which, incidentally, are to be found some of the stories from the Hitopadesa, told with Arabic ornamentation); it is found in Spenser's *Faerie Queene,* the sixteenth-century romance about King Arthur and his knights; and it is used in *The History of Reynard the Fox,* a classic in many languages.

The Hitopadesa and its predecessor, the Panchatantra, have given mankind a number of fables of everlasting delight, and they have given the world's literature an inspiring device which authors have used ever since.

How long ago the Hitopadesa fables were gathered, and by whom, we really do not know. The oldest version gives the name of the author or compiler as Narayana; and a manuscript of this book dated A.D. 1373 exists in India. There is reason to believe that the manuscript of the Hitopadesa we now have is merely the oldest version to survive, but that the contents are actually many centuries older, and that the record of the name or names of the original fabler or fablers has been completely lost.

The Book of Good Counsel ends with:

May the good always be free from misfortune!
And may the glory of the doers of good deeds forever increase!

THE HERMIT AND THE MOUSE

In the forest of Gautama there lived a hermit who was called Mighty-in-Prayer, because whatever he prayed for came to be.

Now one day, as the good hermit sat eating his evening meal, he saw a defenseless little mouse fall at his feet from the beak of a crow. The kind hermit picked the creature up in the palm of his hand. He calmed it and warmed it and fed it with grains of wild rice. Then he found a comfortable place for the little mouse in his hermitage; and there the grateful foundling lived happily for some time.

But one day the good hermit saw a strange cat prowling about his place, chasing the poor little mouse, ready to devour him. Whereupon the hermit prayed, and the mouse instantly turned into a large fat cat. And the strange prowler ran off as fast as he could.

The hermit took good care of his cat, and all went well

until one day a dog came into the neighborhood and chased the poor cat up a tree. There was the dog sitting patiently at the foot of the tree; and up there in the branches was the frightened cat, not daring to come down. The hermit prayed, and instantly the cat turned into a huge dog, so big that none of the other dogs dared harass him.

The dog lived happily with the hermit, until he wandered off into the forest one day and came upon a tiger. The dog was petrified with fright when he saw the fearful beast. But the kind hermit prayed, and instantly the dog took the form of a magnificent tiger.

The hermit still treated the tiger with the same kindness as when he was a helpless little mouse. But the mouse-turned-tiger began to think: "Only the hermit knows that I am really a mouse-turned-tiger. If I should kill him, my secret would die with him."

And so he stealthily approached the holy man one night, intent upon killing him in his sleep. But the hermit was not asleep. He saw the animal coming toward him and knew what was in the tiger's mind. And he quickly prayed: "May he turn into a mouse again!"

Instantly the great tiger turned again into a puny little mouse.

THE LONG-EARED CAT AND THE VULTURE

High in the Himalaya Mountains, on the very top of Vulture Peak, there grew a gnarled old fig tree, its large scalloped leaves flecked with orange and its silvery trunk branching low to the ground. In the hollow of that trunk lived a vulture named Jaradgava.

The vulture was very old. He had lost his eyesight and he had lost his claws. He would have perished of hunger if the birds who dwelt in the same tree had not taken pity on him. Every day each bird brought a little of his own food to the old vulture. Each bird gave him very little. But one and one makes two, and two and two makes four. And when all the birds had brought their offerings the vulture received enough to live on. In return for their kindness, the vulture took care of their young nestlings while the parents were out foraging for food.

Jaradgava took good care of the young birds and never let evil befall them.

One day Long-Ears the Cat came to Vulture Peak in search of prey. As the cat neared the fig tree, the nestlings began to clamor in alarm.

"Who is this that comes?" screeched the old vulture in the tree trunk.

Long-Ears was frightened by the sight and sound of the vulture; but he had come too near to make his escape. He therefore replied in a silken voice: "Master, I salute you! I am Long-Ears the Cat."

"Depart at once," the vulture commanded, "or I shall put you to death!"

"Hear me first, master," Long-Ears pleaded. "Then if you think I deserve death, I will accept my fate without complaint."

"A cat is the enemy of birds," said the vulture.

"Is everyone to be punished or respected only according to his birth?" Long-Ears asked piously. "True, I am a cat. But I live on the banks of the sacred Ganges, in which I bathe daily, and I eat no meat."

"Then what are you doing here?" the vulture demanded.

"The birds that come to bathe in the Ganges forever sing your praise, saying that you are most learned and wise," answered Long-Ears, as he came a little nearer the trunk of the tree. "And so I decided to come and learn wisdom from you, believing that you would not refuse me. For it is written: *The moon withholds not its light from the hovel of the outcast.*"

"Well spoken," said the flattered old vulture. "But young birds dwell in this place and cats love to eat them."

Long-Ears touched the ground with both his ears, and said: "In my sinful youth I was told that the one who eats the flesh of another should observe the difference between the two: the eater's pleasure lasts only a short while; but the eaten is killed forever. It was then that I freed myself of the passion for young pigeons. Now I cannot understand why anyone would want to commit such crimes for the sake of the stomach, which can be satisfied with vegetables which grow wild in the woods."

The vulture was convinced and allowed Long-Ears to come into the hollow of the fig tree.

After a little time, Long-Ears began to kill the young birds and bring them into the hollow of the tree, where he devoured them.

The blind old vulture could not see what was going on.

But the alarmed parents, whose offspring were disappearing from their nests, began to search everywhere.

Crafty Long-Ears realized that it was time for him to leave. He slipped out of the tree trunk and hastened down from Vulture Peak to his own home.

The sorrowing parents continued their search, until they discovered the bones of their young ones in the hollow of the tree. They concluded that the vulture, whom they had trusted, had eaten their young. And old Jaradgava, who had succumbed to the cat's flattery, was put to death.

THE LION OF HARD-TO-PASS FOREST

In the south of India, near the Krishna River, there lived a very wealthy merchant. But instead of looking down and seeing all those who were poorer than himself, he looked up at all those who were richer than he was, and that made him feel poor and unhappy.

"When a man is satisfied with his lot," thought the merchant, "Providence will not better it for him. It is every man's duty to try to increase what he has already accumulated. For if he does not increase it, Providence will surely decrease it."

Having thought this out, the merchant bought a pair of bullocks, loaded his cart with valuable goods, and started out on a trading expedition to Kashmir, far to the north.

On his journey the merchant had to make his way through Hard-to-Pass Forest. And there one of his bullocks stumbled and broke a leg.

"Dismay is the stumbling block of success," thought the

merchant. "I shall therefore not allow myself to be dismayed. If I cannot reach Kashmir with two bullocks, I shall reach it with one. I shall leave the injured bullock behind, go on to Kashmir to make my fortune."

What happened to the merchant, and whether he ever reached Kashmir, we do not know. But we know what happened to the bullock he left behind, whose name was Sanjivaka.

The bullock's leg healed. He found plenty of good food in the forest and grew fat and contented. One day he felt so good that he let out a great bellow, and his voice, like a trumpet blast, echoed and re-echoed through the entire forest.

Now, Hard-to-Pass Forest was ruled by Tawny the Lion, who was king because of his fearlessness and great strength. One day the King of Hard-to-Pass Forest was thirsty and went down to the river for a drink. But as he drew near, he heard a blare like a thunderclap announcing the world's end. King Tawny stopped and listened, then timidly retreated to his dwelling. And there he remained, fearfully wondering what the frightening sound could be and where it came from. For he knew that it did not come from the sky.

King Tawny's behavior was noticed at a distance by the jackal twins Karataka and Damanaka, sons of the king's chief adviser.

Said Damanaka: "Brother, did you notice the master in want of water yet fearing to approach to drink?"

"I saw what you saw," answered Karataka, "and it is our duty to help our king. But as his servants we are at a disadvantage. If we remain silent, we are accounted fools; if we show skill in talk, we are considered prattlers; if we are patient, the king thinks we are timid; and if we are bold, we are considered conceited and ill-bred. Whatever we do, our position is difficult. Now the king is thirsty but dares not drink. What business of ours is that? For if we try to help him, he will only consider us meddlers!"

"No one gains distinction in the service of the king," said his twin brother, "excepting by his actions. Our master sits

timidly before his dwelling and I can see that he is afraid. Let us go and find out the cause of his fear."

"What will you say to him?" asked Karataka.

"I shall decide what to say after I find out whether the king is pleased or displeased with our intrusion."

"Then go to him yourself," said Karataka. "And may your action be according to your wishes!"

Damanaka approached King Tawny and bowed before him. Then he waited until the lion noticed him.

"Worthy Damanaka, wise son of our chief minister, why are you here?" asked Tawny the Lion.

"Your Majesty, I have a question to ask," said Damanaka. "Pray tell me why does my lord, though thirsty, refrain from drinking, as if dismayed?"

"I am dismayed," said the lion, "for I have heard in the forest the voice of a strange creature or demon which, judging by its voice, must be immense and mighty. And because of this demon we may have to abandon the forest. That is why I am dismayed."

"Your Majesty," said Damanaka, "you have cause for misgivings; for we, too, heard the terrible voice. But no one should trust a minister who at the first sign of danger advises his king to abdicate and run away."

"Friend Damanaka," said the king, "a great fear disturbs me, or I would not confide in you that I am ready to give up the pleasures of royalty and go elsewhere."

"My lord," said the jackal, "let me and my brother try to help you. For in time of misfortune, a combination of minds is the strongest shield against danger. Let us try to find out something about the enemy. When we know more about him, my brother and I may be able to devise a way to defeat him."

The grateful king gave the jackal a gift for himself and his twin brother.

"How is it that the king has honored us with a gift?" asked Karataka in surprise when his brother returned. "And ought we to accept his gift, since we do not know the source of his danger and cannot render him any service?"

"Hold your peace, brother," said Damanaka. "I know the cause of the king's fear. It is just a young bullock, abandoned in the forest, who bellowed. And bullocks are food for jackals. How much more so for mighty lions!"

"If you knew all this," said Karataka, "why did you not tell the king and dispel his alarm at once?"

"Because," said Damanaka, "had I dispelled the master's fear on the spot, would he have given us a gift?"

The jackal twins then went deep into the forest until they found Sanjivaka, the abandoned bullock. Karataka seated himself in the shade of a tree in the dignified manner of the chief minister's son. And Damanaka addressed the bullock:

"Oh, Bull! King Tawny the Lion, ruler of Hard-to-Pass Forest, has appointed me guardian of this area. If you wish to remain in this forest, you must make obeisance to our monarch, or else you must depart at once far beyond its boundaries. If you fail to do so, General Karataka, who is with me, will take you to the king, and I do not know what he will do with you in his anger."

Sanjivaka replied: "I like this forest and wish to stay here, and I shall be glad to make obeisance to your king."

All three went toward the lion's lair. After leaving the bullock at some distance, Damanaka approached Tawny the Lion and said: "Your Majesty, we have found the enemy and he is of enormous strength. But we have convinced him to come and make peace with you!"

They brought Sanjivaka before the lion. And the king granted him the right to live in peace in Hard-to-Pass Forest in return for his loyal services.

To show his gratitude to the twin jackals, the king put them in charge of his meat treasury.

After some time had passed Sanjivaka came to the king and asked: "Sire, where is the meat of the deer you killed this day?"

The king replied: "The twin jackals would know, for they are in charge of the meat."

"Your treasurers, the jackals, eat, and waste, and give away each day as much as you can kill," complained the bullock, "and your meat treasury is forever empty."

"That is true," said the king.

"A trusted minister, O King," said the bullock, "should be like a narrow-necked bottle: taking in much and letting out little. But your ministers, the jackals, are like funnels: no matter how much you put in at the top, they let it all out at the bottom. That is wholly wrong."

"You, my friend," said the lion to the bullock, "are a grain eater. You will not waste my food. Therefore I now place you in charge of the meat treasury."

From then on the king's treasury was always well stocked; and the friendship between Tawny the Lion and Sanjivaka the Bullock grew as strong as a bond of kinship.

But the jackals did not like the new state of affairs, and they took counsel with each other.

"The fault is our own," said Karataka. "For we brought about the friendship between them."

"By my wits I made them friends," said Damanaka, "and by my wits I shall make them enemies."

"Then go to the task," said Karataka, "and may you be successful."

Damanaka went to the king and said: "Your Majesty, it is my sad duty to report to you what I consider a great misfortune. For when a minister sees danger, he must offer good counsel in time."

"Speak on," said the king, "and speak plainly."

"This Sanjivaka whom you trust, acts in an unseemly manner and shows contempt for the three powers of Your Majesty: Your Grandeur, Your Strength, and Your Wisdom. It is even rumored that he aspires to your kingdom."

Said the lion: "My good friend, I have a great affection for Sanjivaka and find it hard to believe that he has turned traitor."

"He has not turned traitor," said the jackal. "It is only his inborn nature. The dog's tail, after being rubbed and swathed and bandaged for twelve years, when set free still returns to its natural shape."

"I shall call Sanjivaka at once," said the king, "and confront him with the charge."

"That, Your Majesty, would accomplish nothing, for the traitor will surely deny the accusation."

"How, then, can I learn if he plots treason?" asked the king.

Damanaka whispered in the king's ear: "If he comes to you with head lowered, with eyes averted, his horns pointed at you as if ready to gore you, then you shall know. And being forewarned, you shall kill him for his treachery."

Then Damanaka went to the bullock and pretended to be in great pain.

"What ails you, Damanaka? Are you not well?" asked Sanjivaka.

"How can I be well when my mind is so burdened and I am so depressed?" answered the jackal.

"What weighs so heavily upon your mind?" asked the bullock.

Damanaka came close and whispered: "Although it is forbidden to divulge the king's confidence, I must reveal to you that the master has turned against you and plans to kill you."

"It is hard to believe this, after all the good deeds I have done for him," said the bullock sadly.

"A hundred kind acts are lost upon the wicked, and a hundred wise words are lost upon the stupid," replied the jackal.

"What am I to do?" asked the disconsolate bullock.

"When death is inevitable without battle, and when there is a chance to live by engaging in battle, the wise decide it is the moment to fight," replied the jackal.

After considering this, the bullock asked: "When I see the king, how can I tell that he means to kill me?"

"That is quite simple," answered the jackal. "You will be able to tell as you approach him. If he glares at you, with ears erect, tail cocked, paw raised and mouth open, then you will know that he is ready to attack you. And that is the time for you to show your prowess."

Damanaka left the bullock and returned to his waiting brother.

"I believe," he said to Karataka, "that a breach between the king and his trusted treasurer has been accomplished."

The next time Sanjivaka came before the king, he stopped

at some distance, lowered his head with humility, and watched the king. When Tawny the Lion saw the bullock with lowered head, he lifted his ears, cocked his tail, opened his mouth — baring his teeth — and raised his paw for action. A terrible battle between them followed, and in the end Sanjivaka was killed.

At the feast that followed, the seats of honor were occupied by the twin jackals, Damanaka and Karataka.

THE BLUE JACKAL

A cunning jackal prowled around one night on the outskirts of a town in the south of India, in search of easy prey. As he snooped about in tubs and barrels, he fell into a dyer's vat full of indigo, and no matter how hard he tried, he could not get out. The crafty jackal finally closed his eyes, filled his stomach with air, relaxed his legs, and made himself appear as if dead.

In the morning, when the dyer found what seemed to him a dead jackal in his indigo vat, he pulled the creature out and flung him onto a rubbish heap. But as soon as the dyer turned his back, the sly jackal jumped up and ran off into the forest.

When he knew he was safe, the jackal stopped and looked at himself. He saw that he was no longer a dirty yellowish-gray, like others of his kind, but a brilliant blue, like the blue of the heavenly rainbow.

"My misfortune," exclaimed the jackal, "may turn out to be my fortune!"

Whereupon he called together all the jackals in the forest and said to them:

"My good people, last night the goddess of the forest came to me and with the magic essence of herbs and plants anointed me sovereign of the woods. Behold my royal color as proof of my words! Therefore, from this day forth no transaction shall be made without my imperial permission, and according to my word shall you be ruled!"

The jackals looked at his royal blue color, and heard his commanding voice, and believed that he was really anointed by the goddess of the forest to be their king. They bowed before the blue jackal, and said:

"As Your Majesty commands, so shall we obey!"

With the support of his kin, the blue jackal slowly extended his power over other animals in the forest. First he lorded over those who were weaker than the jackals; then he slowly began to bring under his rule even those animals that were stronger than his kind. He lived in royal fashion by the tribute brought to him, and surrounded himself with old lions and worried tigers and other animals of high rank.

As time went on, the king of the forest became ashamed of being a jackal. He removed all his kin from high office and replaced them with animals of the highest rank, such as tigers, lions and cheetahs. And before those he pretended that he was not a jackal at all, but a sacred animal chosen by the heavenly powers. The jackals, of course, were indignant. But they did not know what to do about it.

Until one day an old jackal said to the others: "Let us not be dejected. It is well-known that the fool who deserts his own kind in order to be accepted by strangers is killed in the end by those very strangers."

"If they kill him, we shall not weep," said the jackals.

"I know how to contrive the ruin of this impudent fellow," said the old jackal. "He pretends he is not one of us and the tigers and all the others believe him because his color is blue. That is why they are willing to accept him as king over them. But if you do as I tell you, they will soon discover that he is a pretender."

That evening the jackals surrounded the royal lair and began to howl, long and plaintively. The king tried hard to remain silent, but he could not suppress his nature and started to howl with the rest. The tigers realized that their king was only a jackal. And they fell upon him and killed him.

THE GIANT ELEPHANT

In the great Brahma forests there dwelt a giant elephant called Camphor-Marks because his front was white. Camphor-Marks was fully the height of three men at the shoulder; his trunk could reach to the top of the cottonwood tree; his tusks could uproot the oak with one thrust; his weight was like that of a mountain; and when he lifted his trunk and blew it like a trumpet, the awesome blast could be heard echoing far in the distant Himalaya Mountains.

The jackals of the forest dreaded Camphor-Marks. They often observed him at a distance and sighed. And they said to each other: "If he were to die, we would be supplied with food for many, many months."

"Why must we wait until he dies?" asked one old jackal, called Sly.

"What else can we do?" asked all the other jackals.

"If we could kill him . . ." began Sly.

The others looked at him in surprise. "Kill him?" they scoffed. "Since when can the flea swallow the tiger?"

"For all his size and strength," said Sly, "Camphor-Marks has one great weakness. Of course we cannot kill him with our might, but we can snare him in the net of his own weakness."

And right there Sly volunteered to snare the great elephant.

The old jackal went to the home of Camphor-Marks. At a proper distance he prostrated himself, touched the ground with his forehead, and said reverently:

"Greetings, Your Majesty! Grant me the great favor of a single glance!"

"Who are you?" asked Camphor-Marks. "And why are you here?"

"I am Sly the Jackal, and have been sent to you by all the beasts and birds of the forest, who are now assembled to choose a king."

"What has happened to King Splendid the Lion?" asked the elephant.

"The king is dead," said the jackal, pretending great sorrow, "and we are now choosing a new king. All the animals, without a single voice of dissent, want you to be our new king. For they know there is no other in this forest to compare in valor and virtue with Your Majesty."

The great elephant flapped his huge ears and said: "I am pleased that the animals have chosen me as their ruler."

"Come with me at once," urged Sly. "At this very moment the animals are waiting to hear from your own mouth that you are willing to be their king. Hurry, Your Majesty! For even more than the rain cloud, the king of the land is the supporter of all creatures. Though the clouds fail, one may live; but not if the king fails."

And saying this, Sly began to walk quickly into the forest, with Camphor-Marks hastening majestically after him.

On their way they came to a great bog. Sly easily ran across it, but Camphor-Marks tried to follow and soon sank so deep in the quagmire that he could not move.

"Friend Jackal," cried out the elephant, "I'm up to my neck in this bog!"

"Perhaps Your Majesty will deign to take hold of the tip of my tail and pull yourself out," the jackal laughed impudently.

Then Sly ran off to call together all the other jackals.

And only then did the giant elephant Camphor-Marks realize how he had been flattered and deceived and trapped.

THE DAPPLED DEER AND THE INTELLIGENT CROW

In the forests south of Bihar dwelt two good friends, a young dappled deer and an intelligent crow.

One sunny day, in May or in June, as the gay plump young deer playfully roamed in the clearing of the forest, she was observed by a certain cunning jackal who was prowling around for prey. "It will be hard for me to get this plump deer if I try to pounce upon her," thought the jackal. "But if I could gain her confidence — oh, what a feast I would have!"

The jackal remained at a distance and called out: "Health to you, O friend!"

"Who are you?" asked the startled deer.

"I am the jackal called Little-Wit. I am a stranger in this forest and lonely. If you will be my friend, I shall be as one who again enters the land of the living."

"If you are so sad and lonely," said the gentle deer, "come and be my friend."

They played in the clearing until the sun began to set behind the western mountains, and then they both went toward the deer's dwelling place.

The intelligent crow in the cottonwood tree saw them coming and asked sternly: "Who is that coming with you, friend Deer?"

"Oh, this is a lonely jackal who seeks our friendship," answered the innocent deer.

"Houseroom ought not to be given to one whose family is unknown and whose character is unproven," said the crow.

Little-Wit spoke up at once: "On the first day you met the deer, your character was also unknown, yet the friendship between you increases from day to day. This deer is now my friend. And because you are her friend, you are also mine."

"No one is a friend or enemy of anyone," the deer put in, "until his conduct makes him a friend or an enemy."

"That is quite so," said the crow. And they decided to give

the jackal a chance to prove himself their friend by his conduct.

The next day the jackal said: "Friend Deer, I know of a field full of corn. Let me lead you there."

He led the deer to a field where the golden ears of corn were just ready to eat. But the farmer saw the deer in his field and that night placed a snare for her. The next day when the deer came again to feed on the ripening corn, she was hopelessly trapped.

"Oh come, my friend, and break my bonds!" the deer called to the jackal nearby.

"Your snares are made of sinews," said the jackal piously, "and I have vowed not to touch meat. How then can I help you?"

And the jackal sat down, waiting for the deer to die.

But when the deer failed to return in the evening, the crow went out in search of her friend and discovered her sad plight. Then she saw the farmer coming into the field with a cudgel in his hand.

"Friend Deer," whispered the crow, "make yourself appear as if dead. Fill your stomach with air; stiffen your legs; close your eyes; and lie motionless on the ground. But when you hear me make a great noise, jump up and run."

The deer did as her friend the crow advised. The farmer was delighted to find his prey dead and at once freed the deer's legs from the snare. But as he started to gather up the net, the crow began to caw loudly overhead. The farmer turned to look up at the crow, and in that instant the deer jumped up and raced away.

The jackal, watching the deer from the distance, quickly followed, intent upon killing her. The farmer, too, turned after the deer, and in his rage threw the cudgel at her. But instead of the deer the missile hit the jackal's head and killed him.

THE CAMEL IN THE LION'S COURT

In a certain forest, there dwelt an old lion called Madotkata the Fierce. He surrounded himself with three friends, a crow, a tiger and a jackal. The lion's friends often went out to scout for food, and if they found prey suitable for a lion, they called their good friend in for the kill and feasted together.

One day the crow, the tiger and the jackal saw a camel in the forest.

"What are you doing here?" asked the crow, the tiger and the jackal in surprise.

"I have strayed from my caravan and am completely lost," the camel replied sadly.

"Come with us," said they, "to our king, Madotkata the
Fierce."

On hearing the lion's name, the camel became very frightened. But when he arrived at the court, the king promised
safety to the camel if he would enter the royal service and become a loyal subject. The camel gladly consented. The lion
renamed him Speckle-Ears and bestowed upon him a title
and a duty.

For some time the lion and his friends lived happily together.

But when the lion became very old and the rainy season
arrived, it became difficult to find enough food for the king's
court. As hunger gripped them, the jackal said to the crow
and the tiger:

"If our master would kill the camel, we would not have to
go hungry. What do we care about Speckle-Ears, the thorn-
eater, anyway?"

The tiger said: "Our king has given him the promise of
security, and a king does not break his promise lightly."

"The king is hungry," said the crow, "and they who waste
away from hunger lose all sense of right or wrong."

The three of them went to the lion and stood before him
in silence.

"Have you brought me anything to eat?" growled the
hungry king.

"May it please Your Majesty," said the crow, "we have
brought you nothing, for we could find nothing."

"We shall die of hunger," mourned the king.

"Our destruction, when it comes, will come because of

Your Majesty's refusal to eat the food at your disposal," said the jackal.

"What food is that?" demanded the lion.

"I mean, of course — I refer to — I have in mind —" and he whispered in the lion's ear: "Speckle-Ears!"

"No!" said the king in anger. He touched the ground with both his ears, and said: "No! That I cannot do! I have given him my royal word of honor! I promised him safety!"

For some time they were all silent. Then the crow spoke up:

"Sire, if the camel should of his own free will release you from your promise and offer himself to you for food, would Your Majesty object to eating him then?"

"I am hungry," answered the king.

The crow then went and found the camel and, under a pretext, they assembled together before the lion.

First the crow spoke up and said:

"Good sir, we looked high and we looked low, but nowhere could we find anything for you to eat. Now, behold, our king is faint with fasting. I therefore beg Your Majesty to break your fast upon my flesh!"

"Good Crow," said the lion with deep emotion, "I would rather die than do such a thing!"

Then the jackal spoke up:

"Your Majesty, I would consider it a great honor if you would deign to make a meal of me!"

"Never!" said the lion, shaking his mane. "Never shall I do such a thing!"

Then it was the tiger's turn, and he said:

"Let my lord eat me and break his terrible hunger!"

"On no account shall I do such a thing," said the lion. "Death would be more welcome than such a deed!"

Speckle-Ears, having heard all the others offer themselves as food for the lion, and feeling safe in the fact that the king had refused to hurt any of them, felt it his duty to do as the others had done. He approached and bowed. Then he started to say:

"Your Majesty, if you want to eat me and break your fast —"

But before he could finish, all three, along with the old lion, fell upon the poor camel.

THE ASS THAT WAS FLAYED

In the City of a Thousand Temples, on the banks of the Sacred River, there lived a powerful washerman named Camphor-Cloth, and his young wife. One night, after a long and hard day's work, when the washerman and his wife had gone to bed and were fast asleep, a barefoot thief slipped quietly across the courtyard and entered the house.

The thief was noticed by the washerman's ass, Worried, who was tethered in the courtyard, and by the washerman's dog, Lazy, who lay sprawled out on the ground nearby.

The ass turned at once to the dog: "It is your business to protect this household from thieves, Lazy. Why don't you start barking to wake the master?"

"My business is not your concern," said Lazy. "You know how well I guard this house. But because no evil has befallen it for a long time, the master has forgotten my services and rarely gives me anything to eat. If his house is robbed, perhaps he will pay more attention to me, his friend and servant."

"What sort of servant and what sort of friend are you, who in time of disaster thinks only of your wages?" asked Worried in anger.

"What sort of master and what kind of friend is he, who rewards his servants only when in dire need of their services?" retorted Lazy.

"You are a wicked wretch!" exclaimed Worried. "It is your duty to waken the master. But if you will not do it, I will."

And thereupon the ass began to bray mightily.

The startled thief quickly came out of the house, without having stolen anything, and ran off. Camphor-Cloth, the mighty washerman, was also awakened by the sound. He looked about him and could find nothing wrong or missing. In a great rage for having been disturbed in his sleep, he came running out into the courtyard with a cudgel and flayed the ass unmercifully.

THE LION AND THE WILY RABBIT

In the mountains of Madura, within sight of the island of Ceylon, there lived a ferocious lion called Hard-to-Tame. Every day Hard-to-Tame went out into the forest very early and killed as many beasts as he could, far beyond what he needed for food.

The beasts of the forest became alarmed. They knew that their king had to eat; but they wished he would stop his wanton killing. Yet they did not know what to do about it. So they called together an assembly of all the animals who lived in that forest to devise a plan which would curb the slaughter by Hard-to-Tame. Finally they went to the lion and said:

"Your Majesty, if you will promise to stop your daily slaughter, we will furnish you each day with a single beast sufficient for your daily meal."

"If you will do that," said Hard-to-Tame, "I promise you, upon my royal oath, to stop killing any beasts."

From that time on the animals of the forest supplied their king each day with his food. One day they sent him an antelope. The next day they gave him a wild boar. The following day he received a parachuting colugo. And so it went, from deer to elephant, to fox, to gnu, to hyena, to jackal — all the way down to quill pig.

Finally the day came for the rabbits to feed the king, and they sent him an old rabbit called Wily.

As Wily went along his way to be eaten by the king, he walked very slowly, thinking:

"I know I must perish and there is no way out, then why need I cringe even before the lion?"

The rabbit took a long, long time going to the lion's den, since he reasoned that the worst that could happen to him was that the lion would kill him, which he expected would happen anyway. By the time he arrived at the royal den of Hard-to-Tame, the lion was tormented with hunger and shaking with rage.

"Why did it take you so long?" roared the lion.

"Your Majesty, it was not my fault," said Wily. "On my way I was detained by another lion, who wanted to devour me. He would not let me go until I vowed to return to him after I had informed Your Majesty."

"Lead me to the insolent wretch who dared detain you when you told him you were on your way to the king of the forest!" roared the angry lion.

Wily quickly ran ahead and led the way to the mouth

of a very deep well. He pointed down into the well, saying:

"There he is, waiting for me."

Hard-to-Tame, inflated with royal pride, looked down into the well, where he saw his own reflection in the water.

"No one dares challenge me in this forest!" he roared.

And he flung himself down into the well and perished.

THE CRANE AND THE CRAB

One day an old crane stood in the shallows of a lotus pond with a very dejected look upon his long face. A crab nearby noticed the troubled look on the old bird, and asked:

"There are fish in this pond. How is it that you stand there as if you have given up the thought of ever eating?"

"I am sad," said the old crane, "because I heard terrible news today. I overheard the fishermen in town saying that tomorrow they will come to this pond and drain it of every fish and every shell to the last periwinkle. When that happens I am doomed, for I shall have nothing to live on. My appetite has left me ever since, and I am now resigning myself to die of hunger."

The fish in the pond overheard the crane, and they said to each other in their distress:

"Since he and we have a common enemy in the fishermen perhaps the wise crane can advise us what to do."

They swam up to the long-legged bird and said: "Sir Crane,

can you tell us how we may save ourselves from this terrible plight?"

"There is only one way," said the crane. "You must get to another pool before it is too late."

"But how can we do that?" asked the fish.

"There is a protected pool nearby," said the crane, "and if you wish I will carry you there one by one."

The poor fish consulted among themselves and said: "Since there is nothing else we can do to save ourselves, we must make an alliance with our foe." And they agreed to let the crane transport them one by one to the pool where they would be safe.

The wicked crane took the fish, one by one, to a lonely spot nearby, where he devoured them. He returned for more, reporting that all the others were now safe and happy in another pool.

Finally all the fish were gone, and the crab said: "Sir Crane, take me also to that pool, for I wish to be with my friends the fish."

The greedy crane, who loved crab meat, carefully lifted the ten-legged creature and carried him off to the spot where he had devoured all the fish. But when the crab saw all the bones on the ground and realized how cunning the crane had been, he thought to himself: "I am undone! Yet when the wise are attacked, even if they see no hope of saving themselves, they still do not give up, but die fighting."

Whereupon the crab fastened his pincerlike foreclaws upon the crane's throat and tore at it until the crane perished.

GOOD-SPEED AND THE ELEPHANT KING

Once upon a time a great drought gripped the land beyond the Nbrudda River. The rainy season came and went, and no rain fell at all. A herd of elephants in the Brahma forest were in great distress, for they had little water to drink and no water in which to bathe.

One day they said to their king: "Your Majesty, how are we to survive? The small animals seem to find places to bathe in, but we, for want of water, are tortured with thirst and discomfort."

The king of the elephants listened to their complaint. Then he led his herd some distance away to a beautiful pool of crystal-clear water. The elephants joyfully stampeded into the pool, and in so doing they trampled underfoot a number of hares who lived along its banks.

After the elephants had departed, those hares which had escaped gathered together in a sad assembly.

"If the elephants, who have discovered our pool, come here daily to bathe," they lamented, "our entire tribe will soon be trampled to death. And yet we are powerless to prohibit them from coming here. What can we do?"

"Do not despair," spoke up one old hare, nicknamed Good-Speed. "I believe I have a remedy for our troubles."

Good-Speed left the assembly and thought for a long time about his plan. "How am I to approach the king of the elephants?" he said to himself. "It is well known that a villain kills by smiling; a king by protecting; a serpent by smelling; and an elephant by touching. I must therefore neither be touched nor seen by him."

Old Good-Speed climbed up to the top of a hill, and from behind a clump of bushes he shouted:

"Ho! Lord of the Elephant Herd!"

"Who are you? And where do you come from?" asked the elephant king.

"Your Majesty, by the command of the Moon God I come to inform you that I have set the hares to guard my pool in the forest. But your elephants came today and frightened them away. That was a great transgression against me, whose title is Sasenka, the Moon Lord, upon whose banner appears the hare." *

---

* The Hindus claim that, instead of the Man in the Moon, they see the image of a hare on the face of the moon.

"Your Worship," the elephant king answered with great reverence, "we knew nothing of this pool belonging to the Moon God."

"Before you are forgiven," said the mock ambassador, "you and all your subjects must come to the pool at midnight. There you will see the Lord Moon floating in the pool and quaking with rage at what you have done. Prostrate your-

selves and ask to be forgiven. Then you and your subjects must leave and never again come near that sacred pool."

The elephant king humbly obeyed. He brought his herd to the pool at midnight, and they all prostrated themselves before the image of the moon reflected in the water.

Then they left and never returned, leaving the hares to dwell in peace.

THE LONG-HOWLING JACKAL

A hunter called Bhirava the Terrible lived in the forests near Kalyana-kataka. One day this hunter, who had lived a long while on fish and fowl, became very hungry for red meat.

"I shall go into the forest," said Bhirava the Terrible to himself, "and find me a tender deer."

He took down his great bow and gathered his arrows and went into the forest to hunt. Near a small pool in the forest he sighted a deer and killed it.

As he was dragging the deer toward his home, he became aware suddenly of someone following him. He turned quickly around, his bow and arrow ready. Only a few paces away a boar of awesome proportions came rushing toward him. The hunter shot the beast through the heart. The boar uttered a roar like thunder, lunged forward, and struck the hunter so hard that the man fell to the ground like a tree felled by a mighty axe.

Some time later a prowling jackal came by and saw the deer, the boar and the hunter, all dead, lying on the ground together. The jackal let out a long howl of joy. Then he thought: "How lucky am I to have come into possession of such wealth!" He sat down and began to calculate: "The hunter should last for a month; the deer should last for two; and the boar will last even longer. Now all the animals in the forest will have to respect me, for I am rich!"

The thought of his sudden wealth had made him forget his great hunger for a short while. But soon his rumbling stomach reminded him that it was a long time since he had eaten.

"How I wish I could keep my treasure intact for a while!" exclaimed the jackal. "Today I shall still my hunger with only that dry gut that binds the hunter's bow."

And saying this, the jackal at once began to chew on the bowstring. Soon the gut was chewed apart, and the hunter's great bow snapped with terrific force across the jackal's breast. The jackal let out just one long howl, and fell to the ground, dead.

LIGHT-O-LEAP AND THE FOWLER

Once upon a time, when night was ended and the moon had disappeared behind the summit of the Western Himalayas, a crow called Light-O-Leap saw a fowler walking through the forest with a bird snare.

In a clearing the fowler stopped, sprinkled rice grains on the ground, and over them spread out the net with its many snares. Then the fowler hid himself in the shadows.

The crow watched with interest to see what would happen.

Soon afterwards a flock of young pigeons appeared, led by their king, Speckle-Neck. When the pigeons noticed the rice on the ground, they cooed in glee: "How fortunate we are!" And they were ready to swoop down to the ground.

But Speckle-Neck detained them, and said: "I do not regard this as fortunate! How do you think this rice came to be in a lonely spot in the forest?"

"How do you, Speckle-Neck, think it came here?" asked the hungry pigeons.

"That grain is like the golden bracelet offered by the tiger to the traveler," answered Speckle-Neck.

"What bracelet is that?" asked the impatient pigeons.

"One day, as I was feeding in a distant forest, I saw an old tiger bathing in a river nearby, rubbing himself with dry grass that he had twisted like a bracelet in his paw. When the old tiger saw a traveler on the bank, he began to call out: 'Ho! Ho! Stranger! Please come and take this golden bracelet!' The traveler stopped and asked: 'How can I come near you, who are known as a killer?' And the tiger said piously: 'Fear not, stranger. For though in my youth I was wild and dangerous, now I am old and powerless and spend my days praying for

mercy and forgiveness for the sins of my youth!' The traveler came closer and asked: 'Where is the golden bracelet you want to give me?' The tiger lifted his paw out of the water, showing the golden straw glistening in the sun, and said: 'Here it is, my good man. Come into the water and get it.' The traveler edged into the water timidly, still afraid of the tiger. As he neared, the tiger jumped at him, and the traveler, trying to escape, fell down. Then the old tiger pounced upon the foolish and greedy man.

"And that," added Speckle-Neck, "is the golden bracelet I mean."

But one hungry young pigeon, looking at the good rice

grain on the ground, said: "Fear can turn even the finest food into poison."

And another pigeon said: "He who never ventures, never enjoys adventures."

Whereupon all the pigeons alighted to feed on the rice. And Speckle-Neck, not wanting to desert his flock, went down with them. They fell upon the food with relish. And soon they were all caught in the snares of the net.

Then the pigeons turned on the one who had advised them to take chances. If their legs had been free, they would have killed him on the spot. But Speckle-Neck stopped their quarrel, saying:

"In time of disaster, dismay is the mark of the coward. Let us rather gather our courage and decide how to get out of this trap before the fowler returns."

"But how can we get out?" asked the young pigeons in distress.

"Let us all, and at the same time, fly up and take the net with us," said Speckle-Neck. "Then I will lead you to a place where our bonds will be loosened."

Soon the fowler appeared and looked happily at all the plump pigeons in his net. But before he could come near, the entire flock rose into the air, taking his net along with them.

Light-O-Leap saw all this happen and followed the pigeons over the range of mountains, curious to find out how they were going to get out of their snares.

On the way, one faint-hearted pigeon turned to Speckle-Neck and cried: "Master, what is going to happen to us now?"

"There are three who will help you in time of need," said the king of the pigeons. "They are: your father, your mother, and your true friend. My true friend is Hiranyaka, King of the Mice, who dwells in these mountains. He will set us free by the strength of his teeth."

The king of the mice lived in a palace, a tiny cave in the mountain. This little cave had a hundred openings, and if he heard danger approaching from one side, he always found an escape to safety through the maze of other openings.

The descent of the pigeons right in front of the Palace-of-a-Hundred-Openings startled the king of the mice. He stood still, trying to figure out which way to run for safety. Then he heard the voice of his good friend Speckle-Neck calling to him. The king of the mice hurried out to meet his old friend and, on seeing all the pigeons in the net, he asked:

"What is the meaning of this?"

Speckle-Neck explained to his friend how they had been caught in the net.

Hiranyaka at once began to gnaw at the bonds around his friend's legs. Speckle-Neck stopped him and asked that he should first free the other pigeons.

"I am old and my teeth are growing weak," Hiranyaka pleaded. "I may not succeed in freeing all of them, and then you, my friend, will remain in bonds forever. I will therefore free you first. Then, I promise you, I will loosen the bonds of all the others as long as my strength and my teeth hold out."

Soon all the pigeons were freed. They thanked Hiranyaka for his merciful deed; then flew away beyond the mountains. And the king of the mice returned to his cave.

Light-O-Leap had seen all this happen, and when the pigeons were gone he came to the Palace-of-a-Hundred-Openings and called:

"Ho! Hiranyaka! How greatly you are to be praised! I saw what you did for your friend Speckle-Neck, and I, too, want to form a friendship with you! Come out!"

The king of the mice did not stir. He called back: "Who are you?"

"I am the crow called Light-O-Leap."

Then the king of the mice began to laugh, and his laughter echoed in all of the hundred openings of his dwelling.

"Why do you laugh?" asked Light-O-Leap.

And the reply came back: "I am the food; you are the eater. What kind of friendship can there be between us?"

THE WAR BETWEEN THE CRANES
AND THE PEACOCKS

1. *The Crane's Report*

In a beautiful lotus pond on the verdant Isle of Camphor, far to the south of Ceylon, there once dwelt a flamingo. He was long-necked and long-legged, swift as a wader and unexcelled as a swimmer. Unlike any other flamingo, his feathers were of silver and his wings and tail were tipped with gold. They called him the Golden-Tipped, and chose him as king of the water birds.

One peaceful day King Flamingo rested on a couch of water lilies, surrounded by his attendants. Suddenly, from an invisible height in the sky, Long-Bill the Crane appeared, floating down in wide circles. At last he came to rest on the pond.

"Welcome, Long-Bill," said the king. "What news do you bring from your distant travels?"

"I bring important tidings, Your Majesty," replied Long-Bill.

"Speak, and we will listen," said the king.

And this is the story told by the crane:

Long-Bill flew far to the north, as far as the land of Jambudvipa, to the top of Mount Vindhya, where the peacock king, Jewel-Plumes, rules over all the feathered creatures — from the wandering albatross to the yellow-breasted wagtail. As Long-Bill searched for food one day, the servants of King Jewel-Plumes came upon him, and they asked:

"Who are you and where do you come from?"

"I am an attendant of the Golden-Tipped Flamingo, Ruler and Sovereign of the Isle of Camphor," said Long-Bill proudly.

"Then what are you doing here?" they asked suspiciously.

"I travel to observe foreign lands for my pleasure and curiosity," replied Long-Bill.

"Now that you have seen the land of King Jewel-Plumes, tell us which of the two countries is better, yours or ours," they demanded.

Long-Bill the Crane sniffed haughtily and said: "What a question! The Isle of Camphor is a province of Paradise. And our king is second only to the Lord of Paradise. To the dwellers of a wilderness like yours it is impossible even to describe my country and my king. But if you were to place yourself under my king's rule, you could come with me and see my wonderful country with your own eyes."

The two servants asked in anger: "Rajah, by whom was that pink flamingo of yours made king?"

The crane replied scornfully: "By whom was that vain peacock of yours made king?"

At that the servants flew into a rage and shouted: "You swamp-dwelling scoundrel who sleeps on one foot for fear of the breeze! How dare you eat our food and at the same time revile our country and our king! For this we ought to kill you!

Why, your king is nothing but a common, web-footed gander. When he eats, he has to turn his head upside down in the mud to scoop up a few insects. How can such as he be a king worthy of respect and obedience? And you, Crane, you are just a frog in the well, and that is why you boast of your country and your lord of nothing-at-all!"

Long-Bill remembered just in time that while modesty is the ornament of the female, patience is the ornament of the male, and he replied:

"You do me wrong. For our king is truly great and so wise that he ought to govern the Three Worlds!"

Whereupon the others shouted: "Come with us and let the court hear this treasonable talk!" And forthwith they dragged the crane before King Jewel-Plumes.

They reported: "Your Majesty, we found this servant of the king of the water birds, from the Isle of Camphor, feeding in our domain, yet reviling your royal name."

Far-Seeing Vulture, the prime minister, spoke up: "Sir Crane, who is the prime minister in your land?"

The crane replied politely: "All-Knowing Duck is our prime minister, and he is famed for his knowledge."

"I would expect a duck to be your prime minister!" said the vulture scornfully.

Then the royal counselor, Sir Parrot, broke in and said: "Why all this talk? The Isle of Camphor and all those other insignificant islands are really part of the Kingdom of Jambudvipa. Your Majesty has only to proclaim that the Isle of Camphor belongs to you, and it will come under your rule."

"How can authority be established by merely saying so!" protested the crane.

"How otherwise than by saying so is authority established?" asked Sir Parrot.

"By war," said the crane.

"Then return to your country," ordered King Jewel-Plumes, "and bid your people prepare for war."

"That is not proper at all, Your Majesty," insisted Long-Bill. "If you wish to declare war on my country, you must send an ambassador for that purpose."

Far-Seeing Vulture agreed that war must be declared through an ambassador, but he added:

"The ambassador sent to declare war must be tested in loyalty, pure of heart, bold, free from any vices, and patient. He must come of noble birth, know the secrets of others, understand the weakness of the enemy and, above all, he must be virtuous."

It was clear that the prime minister thought he was describing himself. The king could see how eager the vulture was for the post, but King Jewel-Plumes said:

"Sir Parrot will be the ambassador."

"I am at Your Majesty's command," said the parrot. "But this crane looks like a villain to me and I hesitate to travel with him."

Long-Bill protested: "Sir Parrot! You know very well that since you come to my country as an ambassador I must treat you as if you were His Majesty the King, whom you represent!"

Sir Parrot replied: "Even kind words accompanied by smiles, when spoken by a rogue, arouse fear in me — like flowers out of season. And I know you are a rogue. Because if there should be war between our two countries, your talk will be the cause of it!"

At the end of his report to King Flamingo, Long-Bill concluded:

"It was then agreed that I should go ahead, and that Sir Parrot should follow closely behind me. And that is all of the news, Your Majesty!"

All-Knowing Duck, who had listened carefully to the crane's report, remarked:

"The crane, having gone to a foreign land, has served the king to the best of his ability — which is the ability of a fool. The wise give in a hundred times rather than quarrel; but contention without cause is the mark of the fool."

"Now what have I done?" Long-Bill complained.

"Even when a fool is a true patriot he can cause trouble for his people and his king," said the prime minister.

"What is done cannot be undone," said the king wearily. "Our problem is to decide what we are to do now."

"The word whispered into six ears is repeated by a thousand tongues," cautioned All-Knowing Duck. "Let us therefore meet in secret to consider this serious matter."

2. *King Crow and Sir Parrot*

When the king and his prime minister were alone, All-Knowing Duck said:

"I am certain this danger of war was brought about by Long-Bill at the instigation of officers spoiling for a fight with our neighboring kingdoms."

"Why should anyone want war?" asked the king.

"Warriors, whose only chance for distinction is in battle, often seek allies in such as Long-Bill to stir up trouble under the guise of patriotism."

"What can we do now?" asked the king, deeply troubled.

"Let us first send reliable spies to Mount Vindhya and obtain a report on the enemy's strength or weakness before we decide what to do."

At that moment the royal chamberlain appeared, bowed deeply, and announced: "Your Majesty, Sir Parrot, Ambassador of King Jewel-Plumes of Jambu-dvipa, stands at the gate!"

"Take the ambassador to the chamber made ready for him," commanded the king, "and I will receive him later."

When the chamberlain left, the king said dejectedly: "It seems that war is at hand."

"It is at hand," said All-Knowing Duck, "but we need not invite it any closer. First we must learn the strength of the enemy through our spies. For who but a lion would go into battle with an elephant? And then we must make certan that our fortress is secure and in order. For although Sir Parrot came here as an ambassador, he will surely report like a spy. Let him report then that our fortress is impregnable."

"There are some in my court," the king complained, "who urge immediate action against the enemy."

"Everyone is a hero who has never engaged in battle," said All-Knowing Duck. "Even when we know the enemy's strength and that we can meet it, I advise Your Majesty against rushing into battle. Entertain Sir Parrot and detain him as long as you can. Meanwhile try gentle means. Spread gifts among the enemy's leaders. Try to sow dissension in the enemy country. Try each method separately and all combined to subdue the enemy; but avoid battle."

Spies were sent out, and the king issued orders for the fortress to be prepared against any surprise attack.

While all these preparations were going on at the Isle of Camphor, Night-Cloud, King of the Crows from Simhala, arrived at Lotus Pond with his retinue.

"The crow is wise and has traveled far," said King Flamingo to his prime minister. "Therefore I ought to see him."

"I wonder why the crow, a land bird, comes to us water-fowl at this time?" reflected the wise duck. "His heart must be with our enemies, who are also land birds!"

"Land bird or water bird, we cannot insult royalty," said King Flamingo sharply. "I shall see King Night-Cloud at the same time that I receive Sir Parrot."

The foreign guests were brought before King Flamingo. They had hardly settled in their places when Sir Parrot, festive in his red, green and blue cloak, cocked his head side-ways and said in a whistling voice:

"O King Flamingo! My Lord Jewel-Plumes commands you as follows: If life and fortune are dear to you, then come at once and pay homage at his feet! For if you fail to do this, you must prepare to flee from the Isle of Camphor!"

"Is there no one here who will silence that traitor?" shouted the king in a rage.

Night-Cloud, the visiting king of the crows, spoke up: "If you will allow me, I will put an end to Sir Parrot."

"Calm yourselves, my friends," said All-Knowing Duck. "An ambassador must not be threatened even though he may be rash in words, for a king speaks through his mouth. Be-sides, who believes in his own inferiority, or the superiority of others, merely on the assertion of a foreign ambassador?"

All the birds smoothed down their ruffled feathers. They talked politely. And when the parrot finally prepared to leave, All-Knowing Duck presented him with valuable gifts and saw him off on his journey home with many good wishes.

3. *The Battle on the Isle of Camphor*

As soon as Sir Parrot returned to the mountain palace of the peacock king, Jewel-Plumes asked impatiently:

"Sir Parrot, what news do you bring? And tell me all about that strange land of the flamingos!"

"The country is indeed like a province of Paradise," the parrot reported. "We should prepare at once for war against the flamingos, so that we may add their beautiful kingdom to our own!"

This idea appealed to the king, and he was ready to declare war. But Far-Seeing Vulture made a long speech advising caution. He spoke of strategy in war and the best disposition of forces; and he displayed his great knowledge of the cost of war for the victor as well as of the losses for the vanquished. He spoke on and on.

"Enough of talk!" interrupted the king. "Let us go out and conquer this desirable land!"

While this was going on, the spies from the Isle of Camphor returned to King Flamingo and made their report:

"Your Majesty, the mountain birds and their king will soon be on their way here. The prime minister, Far-Seeing Vulture, advised caution, but King Jewel-Plumes would not listen to him. We have also found out that one of their spies is now in our midst."

"I wonder who that can be?" said the king.

"That must be Night-Cloud the Crow!" said All-Knowing Duck. "I suspected him at once because he is a stranger and not a water bird. In time of war strangers are to be suspected!"

"But he is the one who offered to kill the arrogant parrot," protested the king.

"*That* anyone would have been glad to do for your august person," said the duck.

"A king flattered by his physician, his priest and his prime minister is soon bereft of his body, his piety and his treasure," laughed the king. "But let us get on with preparations to meet the approaching enemy."

"I believe we can defeat our enemy," said All-Knowing Duck, "for you have heard our envoy say that King Jewel-Plumes disregarded the advice of his prime minister, the vulture. And a war leader who will not listen to the advice of the experienced is easy to defeat. Therefore I advise Your Majesty not to wait until the enemy arrives, but rather to send out our army to slay the enemy before he reaches our own land."

All-Knowing Duck's advice was followed. The flamingo army took by surprise the army of the peacocks and killed great numbers of them.

In his despair the peacock king turned to the vulture for advice.

Far-Seeing Vulture said: "What counts in war is winning the last battle. Therefore, though our forces are depleted, let us not retreat. Our army should advance boldly on King Flamingo's fortress and blockade the gates."

The water-bird spies at once brought word to King Flamingo that though the enemy forces had been severely shaken by their first defeat, they were advancing to storm the fortress on the Isle of Camphor.

"Fear not, Your Majesty," said All-Knowing Duck. "Separate the efficient from the deficient in your forces; and stimulate the loyalty of those worthy by great gifts from the royal treasury."

"Is such an expenditure really necessary?" asked the king, who was very fond of the royal treasury.

"On eight occasions, O King, there cannot be too much expenditure," answered the duck. "And one of them is when an enemy must be destroyed!"

"Then let the expenditure be made," said the king.

4. *The Betrayal*

All was going well for King Flamingo and his subjects when King Night-Cloud appeared and said: "I beg Your Majesty's permission to go out with my guard and prove my devotion to you!"

The wise duck, who still did not trust the crow, put in: "An alligator, dangerous as he is, becomes powerless when he leaves his fortress, the water."

The king did not heed the duck's advice. He permitted Night-Cloud and his retinue of crows to leave the fortress and show their valor.

Early next morning before the sun appeared, Night-Cloud and his crows flew out of the fortress and threw flaming torches on it. And as the fire began to spread, the crows circled aloft, cawing:

"The fortress has fallen! The fortress has fallen!"

The flamingo soldiers, wakened from their sleep, rushed out to see their homes blazing and their fortress going up in smoke, and they hastily retreated to the pond. Then the peacock armies swooped down upon them, surrounding King Flamingo and his warriors. A fearful battle followed, in which General Cock of the peacock army grievously wounded the flamingo king with his spurs.

King Jewel-Plumes entered the fortress of the Isle of Camphor. He stripped it of all its treasures; and then he held court to receive congratulations on his victory from his generals and advisers.

The conquest was completed. The mountain birds flew back with their king to Jambu-dvipa, singing songs of victory all the way home.

5. *The Crow's Reward*

After the confusion of disaster and defeat, after the water birds of Camphor Isle had slowly settled down to their normal lives, the flamingo king asked All-Knowing Duck:

"Who put fire to our fortress and our homes? Was it an enemy or a disgruntled water bird?"

"Look about you, my lord," said All-Knowing Duck. "Can you see any trace of King Night-Cloud and his retinue?"

"On reflection," said the king, "I have not seen Night-Cloud or any of his crows since before the fire."

"If it please Your Majesty, there is your answer!"

"It was our misfortune to have trusted him," said the king.

"Not so, my lord," said the duck. "It ill befits the wise to blame destiny or fortune when adversity befalls him; instead he should rather examine his own errors which led him into that state. As you well know, my lord, I distrusted Night-Cloud from the start and warned you against him."

"Of course, you only guess that Night-Cloud betrayed us, but you have no proof," said the king.

Just then Long-Bill the Crane arrived to report on his secret visit to the land of the enemy.

And this is what Long-Bill reported:

After burning the fortress and homes on the Isle of Camphor, Night-Cloud flew to the palace of the peacock king and was received with great honor.

The peacock king asked the king of the crows: "How could you dwell so long among enemies, Night-Cloud? How did you manage to deceive them?"

The crow replied: "The current of a river, even while it washes the roots of a tree, cuts it down. Besides, there was another thing in my favor, and that was King Flamingo himself."

"How is that?" asked the peacock.

"King Flamingo is high-minded, truthful, and good. And how goes the saying? 'The good think evil slowly and soon forget it.' Though his prime minister, All-Knowing Duck, distrusted me from the very beginning, I managed to deceive the king and made him my ally."

Jewel-Plumes, there and then, wanted to reward the crow for his services by giving him the title of Rajah of Camphor Isle. But Far-Seeing Vulture interposed and said:

"O King, that would not be proper! For although the king of the crows worked as our ally, he did an ignoble thing in betraying those who trusted him. And favor to the base is like writing on the sand at the seashore. Let some other favor be conferred upon the crow."

"Well then, Night-Cloud shall be the Viceroy of Camphor Isle," said the king. "He will take charge of collecting from that island all its fine products, so that we can live in great splendor."

"My lord," said Far-Seeing Vulture with a smile, "he who spends his wealth before it is secured is like the Brahman in the potter's shop."

"Which Brahman is that?" asked the king.

6. *The Brahman in the Potter's Shop*

"There was once a Brahman," the vulture related, "who was given a bowl full of barley one day. He took his great gift to a potter's shop to exchange it for some pots. Since the potter was away, the Brahman sat down and began to think: 'If I can sell this barley to the potter for ten cowries, I shall buy some pots from him. Then I shall go out and sell the pots at a profit. With that money I shall buy some betel nuts and sell them at a profit. That I shall do again and again, until I have enough money to buy a length of fine cloth. I shall sell the cloth at a good profit. And so I shall carry on until I amass a great fortune amounting to a lakh of rupees in gold. Then, being so rich, I shall marry four wives, and one of them shall be very young and very beautiful. Of course, the other wives would become jealous, but when they show their jealousy, I shall thrash them with my cane like this — and like this —'

"And the Brahman swung his cane right and left, breaking his own barley dish as well as some other dishes in the shop. At that moment the potter returned, and when he saw what had happened to his dishes, he caught the Brahman by the throat and shook him with rage. Then he threw him out of his shop."

Then Far-Seeing Vulture concluded: "Therefore, I say that he who spends wealth before it is secured is like the Brahman in the potter's shop."

7. *The Vulture's Advice*

King Jewel-Plumes's feathers ruffled as he listened to the
story of the Brahman in the potter's shop, and he said with
annoyance:

"Then what is *your* advice, my prime minister?"

"My advice," said Far-Seeing Vulture, "is for us to return
to Camphor Isle and make peace with King Flamingo. We
have gained renown for our victory. Now it is time for us to
make an ally of our former enemy." Then he added: "Peace
is a better thing than war."

"Why then was this advice not given to me before we went
to war?" demanded the king.

"This war was undertaken without my approval," replied
the vulture. "Once begun, there was nothing for me to do
but support it toward victory. But now we have learned out
of the mouth of Night-Cloud that King Flamingo is high-
minded, truthful and good. So good a king must have many
friends. If we continue to war upon him and to harass him
and to plunder his country, his friends will come to his defense. Then we will really be in trouble. Therefore I advise
that we should conclude a peace with him."

All this, Long-Bill the Crane related in his report to King
Flamingo.

When the crane had finished, All-Knowing Duck said:
"Long-Bill, I want you to return to Jambu-dvipa at once and
find out how the vulture's advice is received in the peacock's
court."

After the crane had flown off, King Flamingo asked the

duck what he thought the chances were of a lasting peace.

"Frankly," said the wise duck, "Jewel-Plumes is too puffed up with victory to listen to the vulture, who apparently really wants peace. Unless, of course, we make the peacock listen to reason."

"We?" asked the flamingo. "How can we do that?"

"Far-Seeing Vulture actually suggested it. He said that Your Majesty must have friends who would come to your defense in troubled times. I advise you to send a secret message to your friend Great-of-Strength the Stork, Rajah of Simhala, and let him stir up an insurrection against Jambu-dvipa."

"Excellent! Excellent!" shouted the king. "You are very wise, indeed!" And he immediately sent a messenger to Great-of-Strength.

Meanwhile, in the kingdom of the mountain birds, Jewel-Plumes refused to accept the vulture's advice to make peace with the water birds.

"We defeated them," Jewel-Plumes thundered. "If they are willing to live under my orders, supervised by my viceroy Night-Cloud, they may remain. Otherwise we shall drive them out of Camphor Isle!"

The peacock went on and on, and the vulture kept his peace.

Jewel-Plumes was still fuming when a messenger arrived with the news that Great-of-Strength the Stork was heading an insurrection against Jambu-dvipa.

"What is that? What is that?" spluttered the king.

The messenger repeated the news.

"I heard you! I heard you!" shouted the angry king.

"This is the work of All-Knowing Duck," said Far-Seeing Vulture with a chuckle. He enjoyed the trick played by the enemy's prime minister, as only a prime minister could enjoy such a trick.

But the king could see nothing amusing in the situation. He shouted: "I shall go at once and tear up the flamingo kingdom as one tears up a radish by its roots."

"Unfortunately, Your Majesty, we cannot start marching now," said Far-Seeing Vulture quietly. "If we do, our rear will be attacked by Great-of-Strength the Stork."

"What else can we do?" groaned the king.

"We can make peace, Your Majesty," said the vulture emphatically.

"Is there no other way?" asked the peacock.

"There is no other way," answered the vulture.

"Then go and make peace," ordered King Jewel-Plumes, sulkily.

When word was brought to King Flamingo that Far-Seeing Vulture of Jambu-dvipa was on his way to Camphor Isle, he said to All-Knowing Duck:

"He comes as a minister and, as you once said about Sir Parrot, he will probably act as a spy."

"Doubt him not!" pleaded All-Knowing Duck. "Sir Parrot came for war; and Far-Seeing Vulture comes for peace. Besides, Far-Seeing Vulture is a prime minister. And you know that when a king wants to send spies, he does not send his prime minister. I believe the vulture is beyond such suspicion on this mission. Does Your Majesty want to be like the swan who thought the reflected stars at night were lily buds and, finding he could not eat them, refused to eat lily buds in the daytime, thinking they were stars?"

"Very well," said the king. "But you must admit that trickery breeds distrust. And they tricked me once with the king of the crows."

"Let us trust Far-Seeing Vulture, for he was against war from the very beginning. Let us receive him with great honor. And let us listen to his proposals."

When the vulture arrived he was received with great pomp and seated at the right of King Flamingo.

"Sir," said All-Knowing Duck, "it will be our great pleasure if you will consider us and our kingdom at your disposal!"

"Your Excellency," replied Far-Seeing Vulture, "there are no words that can express my gratefulness. But I have come to conclude a peace and not to claim your kingdom." Then he said to the king, "With your permission, Your Majesty, let us consider the terms of the peace."

"How many modes are there to conclude a peace?" asked the King.

"There are sixteen, Your Majesty," replied Far-Seeing Vulture. Then he enumerated all of them:

He mentioned the peace between a very weak nation and a very strong nation, in which the weak nation must accept whatever terms are offered.

He mentioned the peace between nations of equal strength, each remaining independent.

He mentioned the peace between nations that wished to

merge their power, and in which one king gave his daughter as a bride to the other.

He mentioned the peace that is decided by a contest between two chosen warriors, the best terms going to the winning side.

He mentioned the peace of concessions, in which one party or both cede territory or property to the victor.

And so he went on, explaining each, and telling of the advantages and disadvantages of each.

"Of all these, which is the best?" asked the king when Far-Seeing Vulture had finished.

"There is no peace like the one called the Golden Peace, which is preceded by an Oath of Truth and followed by the Bond of Friendship."

"That is the peace we should conclude," said All-Knowing Duck.

They exchanged gifts and good wishes, and then Far-Seeing Vulture returned home. Great-of-Strength the Stork took down the flag of insurrection. And all the birds lived in peace and friendship.

Four

THE BOOK OF
BUDDHA'S
BIRTH-STORIES
(The Jatakas)

THE JATAKAS

Nearly a third of the Buddhist scriptures is devoted to stories, fables and anecdotes about the many incarnations of the Buddha, who, before he became the Buddha, was called the Bodisat. This work is universally known as the Jatakas, or the Buddhist Birth-Stories, and is generally referred to as The Five Hundred and Fifty Jatakas.

Why the number five hundred and fifty is given remains a mystery. For the collection contains two or three thousand tales and fables. Nor does the number represent the cycle of the Bodisat's different births. When the rebirths are carefully tabulated — how many times the Bodisat appeared as a king, how many times as a teacher, a lion, and a monkey, down to his appearance as a jungle cock — the total adds up to five hundred and thirty.

The Jatakas differ in form from either The Book of Five Headings or The Book of Good Counsel. They are not intended to teach princes and nobles how to govern; and the fables or stories are not presented in the "Chinese-nest" fashion. They are told separately, and each one is introduced by telling where the Bodisat appeared and in what form. Usually a definite situation is presented, such as the Bodisat appearing as a minister to a very talkative king. This is followed by the fable of what happened to a talkative tortoise when two wild ducks tried to carry him to their home on a stick. Then comes the conclusion, which is the lesson taught by the Bodisat.

The introduction and story are generally presented in prose; the conclusion is given in one or more verses.

Many of the fables found in the Jatakas are similar to fables found in other collections. This has led some scholars to believe that the Jatakas is the oldest of all the Hindu collections of fables. Others have concluded that the Jatakas came much later and adopted a number of legends already well known in India by the time Buddhism arose.

In the following pages a group of Jatakas are given. They are all in the form of animal fables, each representing an episode in the life of the Bodisat. In some instances two or more fables, or different versions, have been combined. In a few, the conclusions are given in verse, freely rendered, to suggest something of the original form as reflected in faithful translations from the original. But all the fables given here were chosen because they have enduring value as good stories.

THE MONKEY GARDENERS

In the royal gardens of Benares, a group of monkeys were allowed to roam and do as they pleased. These monkeys were great mimics. If the king came by, strolling along one of the paths, they would line up and walk behind him, just as straight and with as much dignity. If the young prince came along playing a game, they pretended they too were playing the same game. Most of all they liked to imitate the gardener. They followed him wherever he went, and whatever his task, they all imitated his motions.

A great festival was proclaimed throughout the city one day, and the gardener was eager to attend the ceremonies. But he had newly transplanted trees in the garden and did not know whom he could get to water them during the day. Then he remembered how well the monkeys imitated everything he did, and he went to their leader and said:

"His Majesty the King bestowed a great honor on you in permitting you to remain in the gardens, where you can feed on all the fruit."

"Oh, yes!" replied the monkey.

"Now there is a great festivity in the city to which I must go," the gardener went on. "To show your gratitude to His Majesty, do you think you can water the young trees while I am gone?"

"Oh, yes!" said the monkey, eagerly.

"But remember, do not waste any water," said the gardener.

"Oh, yes!" the monkey assured him.

The gardener went off to the festivities. The monkeys went happily to work and gathered together all the waterskins. They filled the containers with water and went right out to the newly planted young trees.

"Remember," commanded the leader, "do not waste any water!"

"How shall we know how much is enough, how much is too little, and how much is too much?" asked the monkeys.

"That is very simple," said he. "First you pull up the tree and look at the size of the roots. Those with long roots need much water; those with short roots need only a little water."

"How wise you are!" said all the other monkeys.

They began industriously pulling up all the newly planted trees, and watered each according to the length of its roots, just as they had been instructed.

At this point a wise man came by and noticed what the monkeys were doing. He asked them why they pulled up the trees before they watered them.

"Because we must water them according to the length of their roots," they explained.

And the wise man (who was the Bodisat) said:

"Like these monkeys turned gardeners, the ignorant and the foolish, even in their desire to do good, only succeed in doing harm."

THE FLIGHT OF THE ANIMALS

Not far from the Bay of Bengal, in a grove of coconut palms and carob trees, lived a short-eared rabbit so timorous that he searched for food at night and rarely left his burrow in the daytime.

One day the rabbit came hesitantly out of his dwelling, looking quickly to the right and to the left of him for any sight or sign of an enemy. Reassured that there was nothing dangerous in the neighborhood, he stretched out to bask in the sun near a tall carob tree.

He lay there contentedly looking up at the oval leaves so densely interwoven that not even a pinpoint of sky could be seen through them. Here and there upon the branches hung the ripening dark-brown, sickle-shaped seed pods, swaying in the breeze. They were a pleasant sight to the rabbit, for he well knew how honey-sweet their pulp was when they began to fall to the ground.

Suddenly, as he lay there, an alarming thought struck the faint-hearted rabbit: What would happen to him if the earth began to cave in? Where would he go for safety? The more he thought of it, the more alarmed he became, until his heart nearly burst with terror.

Just then, behind his head a ripe coconut fell upon a dry palm leaf with a thundering crash. The rabbit jumped up in panic without a single look behind and scampered off as fast as his legs could carry him.

As he ran he passed a long-eared hare.

"Where are you running so fast?" called out the hare.

But the rabbit dared not pause to answer. The hare caught up with him and ran alongside, repeating his question.

The fleeing rabbit panted: "The earth is caving in behind us!"

The hare, just as frightened, followed the short-eared rabbit, and soon they were joined by hundreds and thousands of other hares and rabbits, all trying to flee from the place where the earth was caving in.

A doe and deer in a clearing were startled by the sight of so many hares and rabbits in flight and asked the cause of their alarm. And when they were told that the earth was caving in, they too joined the stampede.

As they fled on their way, they encountered a rhinoceros, who asked the same question and received the same answer. And he, too, joined them.

Before long the stampede included bears and elks, wild oxen and gnus, jackals and monkeys, tapirs and camels, tigers, and even elephants.

A young lion at the foot of a mountain saw the animals in flight. He climbed to the top of a high rock and roared three times, his voice reverberating through the valley like a clap of thunder. All the animals stopped in their tracks. They were more frightened by the roar of their king than by the fear of the earth breaking up behind them.

"Why are you all running away?" asked the king of the beasts (who was really the Bodisat in the form of a young lion).

"The earth is caving in behind us," they all replied together.

"Who saw it caving in?" asked the lion.

"Ask the tigers, they know," replied the elephants.

But the tigers said: "We didn't see it, but the wild boars told us so."

And the wild boars said: "We didn't see it, but the camels know all about it."

And the camels pointed to the tapirs, who pointed to the deer, who pointed to the hares, who pointed to the rabbits.

When the lion questioned the rabbits one by one, he finally came to the short-eared rabbit who had started the flight of the animals.

"Are you the one that saw the earth cave in?" asked the lion, fixing his fierce eyes upon the little rabbit, who was now more terrified than ever.

"Y-y-yes, Your Majesty," stuttered the rabbit.

"Where did you see this?" asked the lion.

"Near my home, in a grove of coconut palms and carob trees. I was lying there in the sun, thinking of what would happen to me if the earth suddenly began to cave in, and just then I heard the crash of the earth breaking up right behind me. And I fled."

"Come, show me the spot where you heard the earth breaking up," said the lion.

"Your Majesty, I am afraid to go near it," said the rabbit.

"Do not fear anything when you are with me," said the lion. "Jump upon my back and I will carry you there."

Together they returned to the spot where the rabbit had basked in the sun. And there upon the palm frond the lion saw the coconut that had fallen and frightened the rabbit.

The lion returned to the other animals to tell them what he had discovered. Then each returned peacefully to his home.

But had it not been for the young lion, the Bodisat, the stampeding animals would surely have rushed into the ocean, and all would have perished.

THE MONKEY'S HEART

In a forest near a curve in the Ganges River, there lived a monkey that thrived on the fruit of the fig tree. He grew big and strong and was chosen king of the monkeys.

Not far from the curve in the river lived a crocodile and his shrewish wife. No matter what her husband did for her, and no matter what treasured thing he brought for her, she was never content and always asked for something else.

One day she noticed the monkey king in the branches of the fig tree, swinging happily from branch to branch. And she said to her husband:

"I have conceived a desire for the heart of the king of the monkeys. When I eat it, I shall be as nimble as he is."

"Good wife," pleaded the husband, "we live in the water and he lives in the trees. How then can I catch him?"

"If you try you will find a way," said his wife. "But if you don't get his heart for me, I will surely die."

"Very well, then," said the husband with a sigh. "I shall find a way to catch that monkey for you."

The crocodile swam to the bank of the Ganges and patiently waited for hours. At last the king of the monkeys came down to the river for a drink. The crocodile lifted his head out of the water and said:

"Friend Monkey, why do you always eat the fruit on this side of the river when on the other side of the Ganges grow mangoes and breadfruit and bananas, all sweeter than honey?"

"What you say may be true," said the monkey, "but the river is wide and deep and I cannot swim."

"But I can," said the crocodile, "and I shall be glad to take you across on my back."

The ungainly creature climbed ashore on his stubby legs, and the monkey jumped onto his horny back. The crocodile swung his long thick tail and steered his snout into the water.

Soon they were out in midstream.

"You are a wonderful swimmer!" said the monkey admiringly.

"I am an even better diver," replied the crocodile, and dove into the river.

When he came up again, the monkey pleaded: "Don't do that again, or I shall drown!"

"Good!" said the crocodile. "You did not really believe that I was taking you to taste the fruit across the river, did you?"

"Then what do you want of me?" asked the monkey.

"My wife wants to eat your heart. If she does not get it, she says, she will die. And so I am taking you to her."

"I wish you had told me this before," said the monkey, "then I would have brought my heart along."

"Do you mean that you monkeys go about without your hearts?" asked the crocodile.

"Of course!" said the monkey. "If we carried our hearts with us while jumping from treetop to treetop, they would burst. That is why we hang them up carefully in the fig trees. And that is where my heart is now."

"Show it to me from here," demanded the crocodile.

The monkey pointed to the ripe fruit of a fig tree on the bank of the river.

"Look closely," said he, "and you will see my heart."

"If you will bring your heart to me, I promise not to harm you," said the crocodile.

"Then take me back to shore and I will get it off the tree," said the monkey solemnly.

The crocodile carried the monkey back. Near the shore, the monkey jumped to the bank of the river, leaped up into the branches of the tree and disappeared from sight.

The outwitted crocodile finally returned home empty-handed. His wife berated him and ordered him out of their home until he had obtained the monkey's heart.

The crocodile started out again and this time crawled out of the water and hid himself upon a rock on the bank, where the monkey passed at the end of each day.

After sunset, the monkey began to make his way home. But suddenly he stopped. The rock in front of him seemed larger than he had ever seen it before. He stood still for a while wondering what it might be. Then he shouted:

"Good evening, Rock!"

Only his echo returned.

The monkey repeated the greeting.

Again there was silence, excepting for the echo.

"What is wrong with you, Rock?" shouted the monkey. "Every night you answer me. Why are you silent now?"

The crocodile thought to himself, "If the rock answers his greeting every night, then I should answer him now." And he called out in his unmistakable crocodile voice:

"Good evening, Monkey!"

"I thought it was you," said the monkey, and he leaped to the topmost branch of a nearby tree.

And the crocodile never again tried to catch the monkey king (who was the Bodisat).

THE FOX IN SAINT'S CLOTHING

One day a fox spied a flock of guinea hens and roosters. He stopped at a respectful distance, balancing himself with great skill on one foot. Then he turned his head up to the sky and opened his mouth as wide as he could.

The fowl noticed this curious pose and came closer to observe him. One cock finally asked:

"What is your name?"

"My name is Saintly," answered the fox without turning his head.

"Why do you stand on one leg?" asked a hen.

"Because my great weight would be too much for the earth to bear if I stood on it with all my four legs," answered the fox, without moving a hairsbreadth.

"Why do you keep your mouth open and swallow the wind?" asked another guinea hen.

"Because I live on air. It is my only food," the fox replied.

"Why do you keep your head turned up toward the sky?" asked a young cock.

"Because I worship the sun," answered the fox.

The guinea hens looked at the yellow skin of the scrawny fox and were convinced that he was wearing the yellow robe of a beggar monk.

"What saintliness!" they exclaimed in awe, and the entire flock paid homage to him.

When they began to leave, the fox announced: "I shall be

here again tomorrow to pray on this same spot, and I wish you would come and pray with me."

The next day the fox appeared in the same spot, and the flock of guinea hens came again to pay their respects and to pray with him. As they began to leave, the fox watched them from the corners of his eyes. When the last of the hens was ready to follow the flock, he caught her with great dexterity, quickly gobbled her up, swiftly wiped his mouth, and returned to his praying pose.

This went on for several days, until the guinea hens began to notice how their number was diminishing. One powerful cock had been suspicious of the fox from the start, and

he decided to find out whether his suspicions were justified.

The next time they came to pay their respects to the pious fox, the young cock straggled behind and was the last to leave.

Whereupon the fox sprang at him. But the cock turned quickly. He flew at the fox and pecked at his eyes, crowing loud enough for all the guinea hens to hear him:

"Now we know the reason for your coming here and pretending to be a saint!"

Back trooped all the other hens and cocks and they pecked the fox to death. Then they thanked the young cock (who was the Bodisat in this form) for having saved the flock from the hypocritical fox.

THE ENVIOUS BUFFALO

On a small farm in southern India there lived a water buffalo named Big Red Bubalus with his younger brother named Little Red Bubalus. These two brothers did all the hard work on the farm. They plowed and they harrowed; they seeded; and they brought in the harvest for their owner. In between the crops they worked the water wheel which irrigated the farm and the garden; and they turned the pump to supply water for the house and pigpen.

When the crop was in, Big Red Bubalus and Little Red Bubalus were harnessed again to turn the grindstone which milled the flour for the family.

Yet for all their labors they were rarely rewarded. They were seldom allowed to bathe in the stream, which they loved to do. And all they were given to eat was grass and straw, or chaff when the grain was husked.

This same farmer owned a pig who did nothing but eat and wallow in the water pumped up for him by the buffaloes. Yet the hog was fed on rice and millet and was well taken care of by the farmer and his family.

Little Red Bubalus complained to his brother: "We, who do all the hard work, are treated shabbily and our master gives us next to nothing to eat. Most of the time we have to go out into the pasture to find our own food. Yet this lazy pig is fed all the time and never does any work."

"Envy him not, little brother," said Big Red Bubalus (who was the Bodisat in the form of a buffalo). And he would say no more.

Again and again the younger buffalo would complain; and each time the older buffalo merely said:

"Envy not the pig."

One day the farmer's only daughter was engaged to be married. And as the wedding day drew near, the hog was slaughtered and roasted for the wedding feast.

Then Big Red Bubalus said to Little Red Bubalus: "Now do you see why a pig is not to be envied?"

And Little Red Bubalus replied: "Yes, now I understand. It is better to feed on straw and chaff, and to live out our lives, than to be fattened on rice only to end up on a roasting spit."

THE FOOLISH JACKAL

Ten times the Bodisat was born as a lion. And during one of these times he was born as a fierce young lion with a great mane who lived in the Den of Gold in the Himalaya Mountains. When he was hungry he would look about in all directions, then roar three times, his voice rolling through the distant valleys like a thunderclap. All the animals that heard him froze with fear; and the buffalo and deer, upon whom the lion liked to feed, were most frightened of all.

The young lion would go out and kill what he needed for his food. Then after his meal he would go down to the river to drink his fill of clear water before he returned to his lair.

On his way home from the river one day, the young lion met on his path a very hungry jackal. The lion came upon him so suddenly that the miserable jackal had no chance to turn and run. He therefore threw himself at the lion's feet, begging to be accepted as his servant.

"Very well," said the lion. "Serve me well, and you will never be in need of food."

The jackal fell behind the lion and followed him to the Den of Gold.

Soon the jackal grew sleek and fat on the lion's leavings. Nor did the jackal have much to do. It was his duty to climb to the top of the mountain, where he would look out for an elephant or a buffalo or any other animal worthy of the lion's larder. Then he would call out at the top of his voice:

"Come forth, King Lion, and show your might!"

The lion would leap out of his den, pounce upon the prey, and always leave enough for the jackal to eat his fill.

After some time, as the jackal grew bigger and stronger on the plentiful food he ate, he also became ambitious.

"In what way is the lion better than I?" the jackal asked himself. "He has four legs, and so have I. He has two eyes, and so have I. He has two ears, and so have I. He is mighty, and so am I. The only advantage he has over me is that whenever I spot a victim, I call out to him: 'Come forth, King Lion, and show your might!' This gives him the courage he needs to conquer. Now, if he were to do the spotting for prey, and called out to me: 'Come forth, King Jackal, and show your might!' I, too, would be able to kill the wild horse, the buffalo and even the elephant."

The jackal pondered on this thought for a long time. Finally he gathered enough courage to talk to his master about it.

The lion listened patiently and said: "I understand how you feel, Jackal. But only lions can kill elephants; nor have I ever heard of a jackal who could kill even a wild horse. Why are you not content with your lot? Do you not feed well on what I provide for you?"

But the jackal slunk off deeply hurt, and he remained depressed. At last the lion said to him:

"Very well, Jackal! I shall let you do as you wish. Come, lie on my couch in the Den of Gold. And I shall climb the mountaintop to look for an elephant for you to kill."

The jackal leaped with joy. He stretched himself out regally on the lion's couch and waited for the call.

Soon he heard the lion roar: "Come forth, King Jackal, and show your might!"

The jackal came out of the den as nimbly as a lion, looked about him on all sides, howled three times, then pounced upon the startled elephant, intending to land upon his head. But he missed his aim and landed instead at the elephant's feet. The infuriated beast raised his right foot and brought it down full force on the jackal's skull. And that was the end of the foolish jackal.

THE OUTWITTED HUNTER

Near a lake in the heart of a forest there once lived a deer swifter than the wind. The waters of the lake were the home of a tortoise with teeth stronger than steel. And in one of the trees whose branches were reflected in the lake nested a red-crested woodpecker with an ivory bill. These three became great friends and vowed never to desert each other in time of need.

Not far from this same lake lived a hunter. And when he tracked the footprints of the deer down to the edge of the water, he set a carefully concealed iron-strong trap made of leather thongs.

That evening the deer came for a drink and a visit with his friend the tortoise. Suddenly he was caught in the hunter's trap. More in fear than in pain he cried out for help. The woodpecker hurried from his nest; the tortoise at once came out of the water; and the three consulted on what they should do.

"You, friend Tortoise, begin gnawing on those leather thongs," said the woodpecker, "and I will go to the hunter's home in the morning and detain him as long as I can. If both of us try hard, we may save our friend's life."

The tortoise started at once to bite through the leather thongs which held the deer captive, while the woodpecker flew off to the home of the hunter.

When the first rays of the sun came over the horizon, the hunter awoke, took a knife in his hand, and prepared to go out to inspect his deer trap. But as he came through the door, the woodpecker flew at his face, flapping his wings, and crying at the top of his voice.

The frightened hunter quickly retreated and slammed the door shut.

"It is a bird of ill omen," said the hunter to himself. For he had never before been attacked by a woodpecker.

After a while the hunter decided to leave through the back

door and so avoid the bird with the ivory beak. But the woodpecker realized he might do just that and, as soon as the back door opened, the sharp-clawed bird flew at the hunter as fiercely as before. Again the hunter retreated into the hut.

Meanwhile the sun had risen high in the sky, and the hunter was tormented by the thought that a deer might at that very moment be held in his trap near the water. He finally took down his bow and arrows and opened the front door. And the woodpecker, seeing him with his dreadful weapons, flew swiftly toward the lake, calling all the way:

"The hunter is coming! The hunter is coming!"

By this time the tortoise had gnawed through all but one of the tough thongs and his teeth felt as if they had been filed down to the gums. When the deer heard the woodpecker's warning, he strained with all his might and snapped the last thong. Then the deer fled into a thicket.

The hunter came running up like a bear to a hive full of honey. But his face fell when he saw what had happened to his leather trap. Then he noticed the exhausted tortoise on the ground nearby. He grabbed him and threw him into a sack which he tied securely to a tree. Then he began to look for the woodpecker, with an arrow on his bow.

The deer saw from his hiding place what had happened to his friend the tortoise. He came forward within full view of the hunter, pretending to be wounded and weak. As the hunter aimed an arrow at him, the deer raced out of sight. The hunter followed. Swifter than the wind the deer ran on just out of reach. But when the hunter fell behind, the deer would stop until the pursuer almost caught up with him. In this way the hunter was led deep into the forest and far from the lake.

Then the deer (who was the Bodisat in this form) darted out of sight and circled back to where the poor tortoise lay helpless in the bag. With his horns the deer lifted the bag, ripped it apart, and released the tortoise. And the woodpecker hopped down from the tree to help.

"The hunter will soon return," said the deer, "and his heart will be black with anger. So you, Tortoise, dive into the lake and keep out of sight. And you, Woodpecker, fly off to another part of the forest for a while. And I, too, shall stay out of the hunter's reach."

Some time later the hunter limped painfully back after his long and futile race. He came up to the tree to take the tortoise home for his dinner. But to his chagrin he found only an empty and torn bag.

And the three friends, a bird on wing, a deer on land, and a tortoise in water, lived a long and happy life, secure in their loyal friendship.

THE OTTERS AND THE FOX

Two otters were fishing one day and had the good fortune to catch a huge pike, three feet long and almost as heavy as they were. The pike put up a great fight and both otters were completely exhausted by the time they landed their fish.

When the pike was safely grounded, the two friends began

to quarrel about how to divide their catch. They could not agree on who should get the head and who should get the tail, and to whom belonged the greater share.

Along came a fox and stopped to listen to their dispute. The two otters turned to him.

"We caught this great pike together," they explained. "But we cannot agree on how to divide him between us. Will you help us make a fair division?"

The fox said gravely: "I have judged many cases like this, and I am known far and wide for my skill and fairness in such matters."

The fox cut the pike in three parts, and asked: "Who saw the pike first?"

"I did," said one otter.

"Then to you belongs the head," said the fox, and gave him the head. He asked again: "Who helped secure the fish on the ground?"

"I did," said the second otter.

"Then to you justly belongs the tail," said the fox, and gave him the fishtail.

"But what of the body of the fish?" asked the otters.

"That is my share for acting as judge," said the fox as he ran off with most of the great pike in his mouth.

When the fox arrived home, his wife exclaimed admiringly:

"My dear husband, how very clever you are! Tell me, how did you, a land animal, catch so great a fish?"

"I caught him without having to go near the water," replied her husband, who was really the Bodisat. "I met two otters who knew how to catch the fish together, but they did not know how to agree together when it came to dividing him. And their quarrel made me a better fisherman than either of them."

THE LION WHO LISTENED TO A JACKAL

Manoja was the name of a young lion who lived with his wife in a lair shared by his parents and his sister. The young lion was a good, obedient son and brother, and he provided for all five of them.

One day Manoja returned from his hunt along a narrow path and came face to face with a jackal. There was no room nor time for the jackal to escape, so he threw himself at the lion's feet and pleaded:

"I have come to beg of you to let me be your loyal servant."

"Very well," said Manoja. "If you serve me faithfully, I shall see to it that you are never in need of food."

When he brought the jackal home, Manoja's father said to him: "Jackals are wicked, my son. It would be wiser not to let him live with us."

"Father," answered Manoja, "this jackal has done no harm and wishes to serve us. Let us judge him by his actions."

And so the jackal remained. He served his master well and received good treatment in return.

One day the jackal said to Manoja: "My lord, why is it that ever since I have come to serve you, I have not tasted horse meat?"

"That is because there are no wild horses in these parts," answered Manoja.

"I can lead you to a place where there are plenty of horses," said the jackal.

And he led Manoja to the banks of a river where a number of horses had been brought to be washed. The young lion killed one of the horses and brought the meat to the den.

"My son," said his father, "those horses at the river belong to the King of Benares. The king has skilled archers, and lions who eat the king's horses do not live very long. Stay away from those horses."

But when Manoja and the jackal were alone, the servant said to his master:

"Your father is too timid for a lion. A lion does not need to respect the king's property. Nothing happened to you when you killed that horse. And nothing will happen to you when you do it again."

The young lion went to the river bank and killed another horse and brought the meat home for the family to feast upon. Again nothing happened. Manoja now fully believed that the jackal was right and that his father was wrong. He went on killing the horses.

When the king learned that a fierce young lion was making off with his horses, he ordered them restricted to their stables. And a skilled archer was stationed on the wall of the tower to watch out for the thief and killer.

That night Manoja came for another horse. Since they were not at the river, he went to the stables. He was too swift for the archer as he leaped over the wall. But when he came back burdened with the weight of a dead horse, the archer aimed his arrow well and pierced the young lion as he tried to clear the wall.

Manoja roared in pain and dropped his prey. The jackal heard the resounding twang of the bow and the mighty roar of the wounded lion. He thought to himself: "My master must have been killed, and a dead friend is not a friend at all. It will be safer for me to return to my old home now."

Manoja was mortally wounded but he managed to get home, and died at the entrance to the den.

His father (who was the Bodisat in this form) said: "There lies my son, who took the counsel of the wicked."

His mother said: "There can be no joy in a son who associates with evil companions."

The sister said: "My good brother lies in such low estate because he would not listen to our father."

And his wife lamented: "This is the fate of a king who followed in the footsteps of a knave."

THE KING AND THE MONKEY

The King of Benares was bathing in a river one day when a strange fruit came floating down on the water.

"What kind of fruit is that?" the king asked his men.

"We do not know, Your Majesty," they replied. "But we will ask the foresters. They might know."

They took the fruit to the palace and asked the foresters to come to identify it.

"This is a rare variety of mango," said they. "It is sweeter and better than any other fruit."

The king cut the mango and gave some to the foresters. After they had eaten it without any ill effects, he gave some to his courtiers. And when they finished eating, he gave some to his wives. Finally, certain that it was not poisonous, the king tasted some himself.

"It is true!" he exclaimed. "I have never eaten a better fruit. Where does it grow?"

"This mango grows upon a rare tree which may be found on the banks of the river several days' travel upstream from here," said the foresters.

"Tomorrow we shall sail up the river," said the king. "And you, my foresters, shall come with me and lead me to this tree."

They sailed up the river and at the end of the fifth day a forester pointed at a tree growing close to the bank, and called out:

"There is the tree we are looking for."

The king and his men came ashore and orders were issued for the tree to be guarded so that no one would touch the ripe fruit, which was to be picked the next morning for the king. Then they made their camp nearby for the night.

Late that evening the men were awakened by a host of monkeys who had come to feast on the rare mangoes. The king ordered his archers to surround the tree and kill the monkeys who dared to touch the fruit he had come all this way to gather for himself.

When the leader of the monkeys realized that they were completely surrounded in the mango tree, he tied the end of a branch around his waist and leaped into the air toward the nearest neighboring tree. He managed to catch hold of the end of a branch with both paws, then ordered all the other monkeys to make their escape by running across the bridge made by his body.

The king watched in amazement as the frightened monkeys frantically trampled over their leader to make their escape.

"One who risks his own life to offer safety to others deserves a royal reward," said the king.

The monkey was brought into the camp. They washed him and anointed his many bruises, and they placed him on a soft bed to rest. After he had rested for a while, the king came to him and asked:

"Noble Monkey, why did you risk your life so that the others might escape?"

"I am their leader," replied the monkey (who was the Bodisat in this form). "While it is the right of a leader to enjoy the respect and honor of his followers, he must deserve that respect by guarding their welfare in time of danger even at the risk of his own life."

The king took the monkey back with him to his palace. And upon the palace gates he ordered his stonecutters to inscribe the lesson the monkey had taught him:

Only he is honored who honors others.

THE PEACOCK'S MISTAKE

At the beginning of time the beasts chose the lion to rule over them, the fish chose the white shark, and the birds chose the golden mallard.

King Golden had an only daughter, named Beautiful Princess, whom he loved above everything else in the world. He indulged her in whatever her heart desired, and when Beautiful Princess was old enough to marry, her father said to her:

"Ask for a boon from me, daughter, and it shall be given you."

"There is only one thing that I really want," said the princess. "I want to choose my husband myself."

"That is unheard of," said the king. "But I made the promise to you, and I shall keep it."

When the king proclaimed that the princess would select a husband, all varieties of birds appeared on the trees and on the rocks and in the clearings of the grounds designated by King Golden.

There were mallards and eagles, swans and owls, parrots

and storks, plovers and ostriches, hammerheads and cocka-
toos, and every conceivable kind of mountain bird and water
bird, big and little, sweet singers and harsh screamers—
each one hoping to be chosen by Beautiful Princess.

As the birds began to parade before her, the princess saw
a beautiful peacock. And her heart began to flutter. His
movements were graceful and his plumage was dazzling. The
color of his neck was a richer blue than lapis lazuli; his
lovely back was covered with shining green and gold; his
proud head was tufted with iridescent feathers that matched
the splendor of the tail which he spread out like a great fan
behind him. Not another bird in the entire assembly was
even remotely as handsome.

"That is the one I would choose to be my husband!" the
princess whispered to her father.

The king announced the choice of the princess.

The peacock was overjoyed with his good fortune. He
spread his wings; he began to dance; and he sang in his dis-
agreeable voice. When he exhibited his lack of modesty
and his unpleasant voice, the princess told her father that
she regretted her choice.

"Then it shall be my turn to choose a husband for you,"
said King Golden.

The king (who was the Bodisat) announced to all the birds
that Beautiful Princess had changed her mind. And he chose
a young golden mallard to join the royal family.

The peacock left as quickly as he could, ashamed that
he had won the princess with his beauty yet lost her with his
vanity.

THE ELEPHANT AND THE CARPENTERS

Many centuries ago, in a certain village near a river in India, all the men were trained as carpenters. All the men, five hundred of them, would go up the river on rafts until they reached the great forests. There they cut the trees, seasoned the lumber, shaped the beams and sawed the planks to be used in building houses.

One day an old elephant sought refuge from the heat of the sun in the shade of the woods where the carpenters worked. As he stepped into a pile of shavings, a long blackwood splinter pierced his foot. His foot began to fester and he was in great pain when he tried to walk.

As he limped along, the elephant heard the voices of men nearby. He followed the sounds and came upon the busy carpenters. They noticed that the elephant was limping, and then they saw the long blackwood splinter sticking out of his swollen foot.

The carpenters gently pulled out the splinter. Then they lanced and cleansed the festering wound.

The wound healed quickly. But the elephant did not forget the kindness of the carpenters. He returned to help them with the hard work of pulling logs from one place to another and in loading lumber on the rafts. The carpenters, in turn, fed the elephant well, each of the five hundred men giving him a portion of his own food.

After the work of the day the elephant would go down to the river to swim, and there the carpenters' children would climb over his back, pull his trunk, whistle into his ears, and play all varieties of pranks on him. The elephant (who was the Bodisat) loved the children and never permitted any harm to befall them.

And the devotion of the grateful elephant became known throughout the land.

THE GRATEFUL MOUSE

Many centuries ago in Benares there lived a stonecutter who was never known to be angry. He sang as he worked, loved his enemies as much as his friends, and showed kindness to all creatures, even to a little mouse that came scampering through his shop.

Now this mouse had made its nest in an underground chamber where, many generations before, a miser had buried his treasure of coins. And the mouse, in gratitude to the stonecutter for his kindness, came to him fearlessly one day with a coin in its mouth, and said:

"I have brought you money, kind sir! Part of it is for you; and with the rest I want you to buy me meat so that I shall not have to hunt for food or touch your cheese."

The stonecutter took the coin and spent half of it on meat for the mouse. The gentle creature took the food to her underground nest and stayed there until it was gone. Then she came to the stonecutter with another coin from the miser's treasury for more food.

This went on for some time, until the mouse came home one day and found a large black cat blocking the entrance that led to her underground dwelling.

"Please go away," the little mouse pleaded, her tail clutching the floor for any emergency.

"Why should I?" asked the cat. "I am hungry. And cats, you know, live on mice."

"Are you hungry only now, or do you get hungry every day?" asked the cunning mouse.

"Of course I get hungry every day," replied the cat. "Why do you ask?"

"Because, if you eat me now, you will be hungry again

tomorrow," answered the mouse. "But if you let me go, I will bring you meat every time you are hungry. The day I fail to do so, you can kill me."

The cat agreed to let the mouse go on those terms. And after that each day the mouse shared her meat with the cat.

But one day a sleek gray cat caught the little mouse. The clever little creature made the same pact with the gray cat. And after that she divided her food into three parts to keep her bargain with her two captors.

But later a third and a fourth cat threatened to kill the little creature. The mouse made the same offer to each of them and they accepted. When the mouse divided her meat into four parts there was nothing left for herself to live on.

The mouse confided in the stonecutter and told him all her troubles.

"Do not fear those cats any longer," said the stonecutter. "I shall help you drive your enemies away."

The old man took a block of clear crystal, hollowed it out like a ball, and told the mouse to get inside. Then he placed the ball near the entrance to the mousehole.

"When you see a cat coming," he instructed the mouse, "start to abuse him and threaten him if he does not leave you alone. Then see what happens."

The mouse waited in the crystal ball. Soon the black cat came for his meat. The mouse told him she had no food for him, and threatened to kill the cat if he tried to come near her. The cat sprang at the little creature, determined to kill her on the spot. But when he pounced on the crystal ball, he shattered his sharp claws. The surprised and shaken cat ran off, never to return again.

Each of the other cats came in turn. And to each the same thing happened.

After that no cat ever came near to molest the little mouse. And the grateful creature came each day with two and three coins for her friend the stonecutter (who was the Bodisat in this form), and they lived in friendship to the end of their days.

THE HAREBRAINED MONKEY

The King of Benares received news one day that a group of outlaws were committing outrages on a distant border of the kingdom. The news angered the king. He quickly gathered his army and started off for the distant border, leaving his kingdom unguarded and without a ruler.

On their long march, the king and his army made camp for the night wherever they could. One rainy day they stopped in a forest, seeking shelter under the trees. They unsaddled their horses and steamed some peas, which they fed to their steeds in long narrow troughs.

A monkey in a tree nearby saw the horses being fed, and he came racing down, filled both paws with peas, then scampered nimbly up to a branch and settled down to eat. But as he opened one paw, a single pea fell to the ground. Without hesitation, the monkey jumped down from his perch to hunt for the lost pea, and in doing so he dropped all the other peas in his paws.

The king observed this foolish monkey and was greatly amused. He turned to his counselor and asked:

"Friend, what do you think of this monkey who would give up so much to retrieve so little?"

"That is the way of the foolish," replied the counselor, who was the Bodisat. "They will give up much that is certain for a little that is uncertain."

Then he added:

And we, great monarch
Are we not like the monkey in the tree?
To gain so little we neglect so much —
Exactly like the monkey with its pea.

The king understood the rebuke and realized how very foolish he had been himself to leave his kingdom unguarded. He issued orders to his men, and he and his army returned at once to Benares.

THE TIGER AND THE GOATS

A group of goatherds lived near mountains infested with panthers and tigers. To protect their flocks from the wild animals, they often drove them into a cave. In the evening they would come and take their goats down into the village to be milked.

Once a billy goat lingered in the cave, and by the time he came out, the flock was already far down in the valley. As he hurried to catch up with them the lone goat met a tiger, moving silently toward him.

"If I turn, I can only run into the cave, and there the tiger will trap me," thought the goat. "There is nothing for me to do but attack."

He lowered his sharp horns, braced himself on his powerful front legs, and sprang forward. The startled tiger was caught off guard and went rolling down the mountainside. In the meantime the goat fled toward home as fast as he could, until he caught up with the others.

When the goat (who was really the Bodisat) told the story of his encounter, some others in the flock wished they could meet a tiger or a panther so that they, too, could show their mettle. The next time the flock was driven into the cave, one young goat in search of adventure deliberately stayed behind. When he came out alone, there was the tiger waiting for him.

The rash goat could not run back; and he could see that the tiger was ready for him and could not be taken off guard. The goat decided to try to disarm his enemy with friendly talk and flattering words:

"How are you, my uncle?" said the goat to the tiger, as if he were a relative he had just met. "Is all well with you and yours?"

"How dare you call me 'uncle' when you step upon my tail?" growled the tiger.

"But I came forward facing you," the goat protested, "and your tail is behind you."

"My mighty tail is everywhere, you silly goat!" roared the tiger.

"That is true, too, my lord," said the goat, his teeth beginning to chatter. "But I was really very careful, and I came down here walking on the air."

"I know you came through the air," growled the tiger, "because you have frightened away all the deer upon which I feed. And for that I shall have to devour you."

"Please have pity!" the goat began to plead.

But by that time it was already too late.

THE CROW IN THE ROSE-APPLE TREE

A crow sat perched on the high branch of a rose-apple tree eating the sweet ripe fruit.

Along came a jackal who hungered for the creamy-yellow rose apple with its entrancing fragrance. But the branch bearing the fruit was thirty feet above him and he could not reach it. As he looked up, his mouth watering, the jackal spied the crow in the uppermost branches eating contentedly.

"If I flatter that bird," thought the jackal, "perhaps he will throw down some of those rose apples."

So he addressed the crow, saying:

> *Who can it be, who sits in this tree —*
> *The sweetest singer of all the songbirds?*
> *See him there, resplendent as a peacock,*
> *Singing with such beauty and such grace!*

The crow, deeply touched by this flattery, cawed back in its unpleasant voice:

> *Only one that comes of noble birth*
> *Can see in others their true worth.*
> *You, below, resemble a tiger to me;*
> *Deign to taste the fruit of this tree.*

And saying this, the crow shook the branches of the rose-apple tree and caused the ripe fruit to fall, to the jackal's delight.

Now the Bodisat (who was a tree fairy at this time) heard the jackal flatter the crow and the crow flatter the jackal, while both feasted on the good fruit of the tree. And he spoke up in a voice so loud that both the bird and the beast could hear him, and he said:

> *Too long, too long have I suffered the sight*
> *Of a carrion crow who can only caw*
> *And a refuse-eater like the jackal below*
> *Flattering each other with dishonest prattle!*

The voice of the tree fairy so terrified the crow and the jackal that both left the rose-apple tree as fast as they could, and they never returned.

THE ASS IN THE LION'S SKIN

An old trader went from village to village hawking his goods, which were carried for him on the back of his faithful ass. At the outskirts of each village the trader would unpack his goods, dress his ass in a lion's skin, and turn him loose in the rice or barley fields. And while his ass fed on the peasants' crops, the hawker peddled his goods in the village from door to door. The watchmen in the fields dared not come near the ass to drive him away, since they mistook him for a lion.

One day the trader stopped at the outskirts of a village and, while he prepared his own breakfast, turned the ass loose in a green barley field, wearing the lion's skin.

The watchmen in the field dared not come near him, thinking he was a lion, but they hastened to sound the alarm in the village. And the villagers, concerned for the safety of their crop, armed themselves with weapons and rushed to the field, beating drums and blowing horns and shouting at the tops of their voices.

When the frightened animal saw them coming, he uttered a great cry — the bray of an ass!

Then the villagers knew it was not a lion that despoiled their field. And one farmer called out:

> *This is not a lion roaring,*
> *Nor a tiger, nor a panther,*
> *But a common wretched ass*
> *With a lion's skin upon him.*

The villagers, no longer afraid, rushed at the poor creature, stripped him of the lion's skin, and beat him mercilessly as they drove him from their barley field.

And the farmer (who was the Bodisat) said again:

> *Long might the ass*
> *Clad in a lion's skin*
> *Have fed on the barley green;*
> *But he brayed —*
> *And at that moment he came to ruin!*

The poor ass died of his beating. And the trader hastily left the village carrying his wares upon his own back.

THE AGE OF THE PARTRIDGE

An elephant, a monkey and a partridge lived as neighbors in a banyan grove. They had known each other so well and so long that they began to treat each other with the disrespect of familiarity. They did not feel contempt for each other, for they were very good friends; but not one of them had more authority than another, and their friendship lacked the honor of order.

They met one day and agreed that they must do something to change this. The monkey said:

"We should find out who is the eldest of us three and to him we will accord the honor due to age. We will come to him in all matters between us and bow to his authority as judge."

The elephant and the partridge agreed to this, but the three animals could not devise a way of determining which of them was the oldest.

One hot day, as they gathered in the shade of a great banyan tree, the partridge suddenly asked:

"Tell me, friend Elephant, how big was this banyan tree when you first saw it?"

"Oh, when I was young," replied the elephant, "this great tree was no taller than a bush. I could step over it and it barely touched my stomach. I remember the banyan tree since it was *that* little."

"When I was young," said the monkey, thinking as far back as he could remember, "I could sit on the ground just as we sit now and nibble the topmost leaves of this banyan tree. It was *that* small."

"Then I must be the oldest of us three!" exclaimed the partridge.

"How so?" asked his friends.

"For, my dear friends, I remember the time when there was no tree here at all!" replied the partridge. "When I was very young, there used to be a great grove of banyan trees some distance away from here. I went there often to feed on the seeds. I remember one day dropping a seed on this very spot. And from it grew this great tree."

The monkey and the elephant conceded that the partridge was the oldest. (And he really was, for he was the Bodisat.) They paid him the respect due an elder, and they consulted him in all matters.

THE TALKATIVE TORTOISE

In a pond in the Himalaya Mountains there once lived a handsomely marked young tortoise. He was not vicious like his cousin the snapping turtle, but he had the failing of liking to talk too much. Two wild ducks came to the pond in search of food one day, and the tortoise started to talk to them almost as soon as they alighted on the water.

Nevertheless the ducks and the tortoise became great friends, and the ducks said one day:

"We have a fine home on Mount Beautiful in the Himalayas, next to the Cave of Gold. Why don't you come and live with us, friend Tortoise?"

"How can I, a tortoise, get up to your place?"

"We thought of that," said the wild ducks. "We can take you to our home, if only you can keep from talking and not say a single word until we get there. Do you think you can do that and keep your mouth closed all that time?"

"I certainly can do that!" the tortoise assured them.

The ducks took a sturdy stick and asked the tortoise to bite hard on the center. Then they each took hold of an end of the stick with their strong bills and rose into the air, swiftly flying toward the mountains.

As they flew over the palace of the King of Benares, a number of village children saw the wild ducks in flight, carrying a tortoise on a stick.

"Look! Look! Two wild ducks are carrying a tortoise on a stick!" they shouted excitedly to their parents.

Their outcries angered the tortoise, and he wanted to shout back at them:

"If my friends want to carry me like this, what affair is that of yours, you wretches!"

But when he opened his mouth to speak, he let go of the stick and fell with great force into the open courtyard of the palace; and he split in two.

The king's attendants came running up in excitement, shouting:

"A tortoise has fallen out of the sky into the courtyard!"

Everyone, including the king and his Brahman and all his courtiers, gathered around the spot where the dead tortoise lay.

The king turned and asked the Brahman: "Teacher! What made this creature fall here?"

Now, this king was very talkative and no one could ever get a word in edgewise. The Brahman gladly took this opportunity to admonish him. He answered:

"My King, his tongue killed him."

The king looked at him in amazement. And he asked: "How could his tongue bring him to his death?"

O King, this tortoise held secure
A stick between his teeth;
But when he tried to chatter
He quickly met this fate.

Behold him, O excellent of strength,
And speak not out of season!
You see how this tortoise fell —
He talked too much and that's the reason!

The king asked: "Are you referring to me, Teacher?"

And the teacher (who was the Bodisat born as a Brahman) replied:

"O Great King! Be it you, or be it another. Whoever talks too much sooner or later meets with disaster."

THE GOLDEN GOOSE

Once there lived a good man who had a shrewish wife and three kind daughters. When the man died, his wife and children were left in need. For although the man was always good, he was also always very poor. Only the pity of neighbors and the charity of friends kept the woman and her daughters from starving to death.

The widow and her three daughters awakened in their cold room one morning and saw a goose resting on the beam of their ceiling. He was a bird of magnificent size, and all his feathers were of pure gold.

"Who are you?" asked the girls in wonder.

"I am your father," said the goose, "for I was reborn in this form. Now you shall know no want. For I will give you one of my feathers and that should keep you in comfort for some time. When you have spent the price of that feather, I shall bring you another, so that you can live in ease all the days of your life."

And so saying he dropped one of his golden feathers down to the floor. Then he disappeared.

With the money they obtained for the golden feather, the mother and her daughters bought fine clothes and ornaments, and all the food they needed.

Each time their funds grew low, the goose (who was the Bodisat in this form) would return and leave another golden feather.

But the shrewish widow became covetous. And she said to her daughters:

"A goose is a goose, and there is no trusting them. What if he should disappear one day and never return? We would be in misery again. Therefore let us catch him next time he comes and pluck him of all his golden feathers. Thus we shall make sure of having enough for our needs as long as we live."

The daughters were horrified by their mother's scheme. They argued that to pluck the good goose of all its feathers would cause him great pain. They would not consent to such a plan.

But next time the golden goose appeared to leave a feather

for his daughters, the widow was at home alone. She caught the goose and cruelly plucked out all his feathers. Then she flung the poor creature out-of-doors.

The woman quickly returned to count the treasure of golden feathers in her basket. To her great dismay, there in the basket lay only ordinary feathers, just like those from any goose.

And the golden goose never visited his family again.

THE UNGRATEFUL LION

One day a young spotted lion named Felix roamed through the mountains for prey. He found a deer, killed it, and started to devour it in haste. But as he ate greedily, a bone stuck in his throat, and he could not get it out nor could he get it down.

The lion's throat began to swell and his pain grew agonizing.

Just then a woodpecker came along in search of grubs under the bark of a tree, and he saw the suffering lion.

"What troubles you, King of Beasts?" asked the woodpecker from his perch on a bough high in the tree.

"A bone is lodged in my throat," groaned Felix. "I cannot get it up and I cannot get it down; and if it remains there much longer, I shall surely die."

"I would gladly try to pull the bone out of your throat," said the woodpecker. "But how dare a bird put his head into a lion's mouth?"

"Fear not, my friend," Felix pleaded. "How can you think that if you saved my life I would ever hurt you!"

"Then lie down on your side and open your mouth as wide as you can," ordered the woodpecker.

Felix meekly obeyed. The woodpecker, still wary of the lion, came down from his perch and fixed a strong twig between the animal's upper and lower jaws, so that the great beast could not close his mouth even if he tried. Then the woodpecker stuck his head deep into the lion's mouth, caught the end of the bone in his powerful bill, and, bracing himself against the lion's mane, yanked it out as if it were a loosened tooth. As the woodpecker withdrew his head from the lion's mouth, he knocked the twig out with the top of his bill, and quickly flew up to safety in the tree. Young Felix, still ill from the wound in his throat, went off to his lair to rest.

Some time later the woodpecker decided to test the lion's gratitude. He flew near the lion's lair, and said:

"King Lion, do you remember how I saved your life by pulling a bone out of your throat? What reward are you willing to give me?"

"I have already given you your reward," said arrogant young Felix.

"Which reward is that?" asked the astonished woodpecker.

"You, a puny feathered creature, dared stick your head into a lion's mouth, and you are still alive to tell the tale. That is reward enough."

And the woodpecker (who was the Bodisat in the form of a bird) said:

"That is what I thought would be the reward for a kindness done to a wretch like you. For the knave always repays a favor with an insult."

THE GREEDY CROW

Long ago, the people of Benares had a custom of hanging straw baskets in their gardens for the shelter of the birds. They padded the baskets with straw, to make them more comfortable, and from time to time they fed the birds with the crumbs from their tables. The birds who lived in these baskets grew very tame. Sometimes a cook in a great mansion would even take the basket into the kitchen to protect the birds from the wind and rain.

One such basket hung in the kitchen of the gildermaster of Benares, where the cook of the household sheltered a pigeon. Each daybreak the pigeon left the basket, flew out of the open window in search of food; and in the evening he returned to his warm and comfortable nest in the kitchen. Here he lived for some time in safety and contentment.

A crow came by one day, attracted by the smell of fresh fish cooking in the gildermaster's kitchen. He perched on the branch of a nearby tree, wondering how he could get into that kitchen to feast on the delicacy. All day long he sat there planning how to get into the kitchen undetected. But he could not think of anything that seemed safe or sound. Then, toward evening, he noticed the pigeon enter the kitchen by the open window.

"If no harm befalls this pigeon," said the crow to himself, "I shall manage to enter next time with him."

At dawn the following morning the crow came back. As the pigeon left in search of food, the crow followed closely behind.

"Why do you follow me?" asked the pigeon.

"I like you," said the crow. "I like your ways and I admire your conduct. I should like to stay near you so that I may learn your good manners."

"But how will you live?" asked the pigeon. "Your kind and mine live on different food."

"Where you seek your food, there I shall also seek mine," answered the crow. "We can feed side by side without competing with each other."

"If you insist," said the pigeon, though still suspicious of the crow.

All day long the pigeon searched for grass seed and wild berries; while the crow by his side looked for worms and insects. At the end of the day the pigeon returned to his home in the gildermaster's kitchen, and the crow followed close behind him.

"Look!" exclaimed the cook. "Our pigeon has brought home a friend of his!"

And he hung up another basket for the crow.

For some time after that the two birds lived side by side, leaving together each morning and returning together each night.

One evening a great feast was in preparation in the kitchen and salt fish were hung up from the rafters. The smell of the fish filled the crow's stomach with longing and his head with tempting schemes. All night long he lay groaning in his basket. And when the pigeon was ready to leave in the morning, the crow moaned:

"My good friend, you must go without me. For I have such a pain in my stomach that I cannot move."

The pigeon looked at the crow in surprise. "I have never heard of a crow suffering stomach pains," said he. "Are you certain you are not sick with longing for that fish hanging from the rafters? For if you are, I can give you good advice: food meant for the master of the house will make your stomach even sicker than it is now. Come, and seek your own food."

The crow pretended to be very hurt because the pigeon doubted his motives; and he repeated that he was too ill to move.

"I must leave," said the pigeon. "See that you do not fall prey to your own greed." And with this advice he flew out of the kitchen.

The cook had meanwhile taken down the fish and dressed them and placed them in a dish all ready to be steamed. The fires were started and it grew very hot in the kitchen. The cook stepped out into the yard to cool off a little. But he was no sooner gone than the crow popped out of his basket, glanced thievishly about him, and knocked the cover off the dish, ready for the feast he had been waiting for so long.

The cook in the courtyard heard the clatter of the falling cover and rushed back into the kitchen just in time to catch the black thief as he prepared to snatch the fish.

"So that is how you repay me for letting you sleep in my basket?" said the irate cook. "Now watch and see how I will repay you for trying to gobble up the dinner I so carefully prepared for my master!"

He plucked out the crow's feathers, doused its wounds with pepper and sour milk and then threw the miserable bird back into the basket.

When the pigeon returned home that evening, he found the crow in real pain and on the point of death.

"In your greed you would pay no heed to my advice," said the pigeon (who was the Bodisat in this form). "Now you must die for your actions. Nor can I remain here any longer. For the cook will suspect me, too, as the friend of a thief."

The pigeon flew away, and the cook threw the crow and the basket on the dust heap, and never allowed another bird into his kitchen.

Books to Read

The following brief list of books, with notes, is presented for the reader who may wish to understand the place of the fable in Hindu literature, or who may wish to examine literal translations of the Hindu fables. Some of these books contain bibliographies, or describe their sources in introductions, and readers can continue to explore the topic as far as their interest will carry them.

BUDDHIST BIRTH-STORIES, by T. W. Rhys Davids; Trubner's Oriental Series, Routledge, London, 1893.

This book presents an abbreviated version of the Nidana-katha, which deals with the Buddha's lineage as far back as "a hundred thousand cycles ago."

CAMBRIDGE HISTORY OF INDIA, in 6 volumes, edited by E. J. Rapson; Macmillan, New York, 1922.

This is a scholarly, comprehensive work, which devotes considerable space to India's literature.

THE DAWN OF LITERATURE, by Carl Holliday; Crowell, New York, 1931.

This good book contains a long chapter on the dawn of Hindu literature; and a particularly interesting, if brief, discussion of Hindu legends and fables.

HINDU LITERATURE, edited by Epiphanius Wilson; Collier, New York, 1900.

This book contains a large portion of the Hitopadesa as translated from the Sanskrit by Sir Edwin Arnold. Sir Edwin attempts to convey in English the feeling and rhythm of the original.

A HISTORY OF INDIAN LITERATURE, by Herbert H. Gowan; Appleton, New York, 1931.

This is a delightful one-volume history of India's literature, from the Vedic times to the twentieth century. The Jatakas and the beast fables are presented in perspective, so that their place in the general development of Hindu literature is readily grasped. In addition, the volume contains a splendid bibliography.

HITOPADESA OR THE BOOK OF GOOD COUNSEL, by B. Hale-Wortham; Routledge, London (no publication date given).

Another translation from the Sanskrit, with an excellent introduction.

HITOPADESA: THE BOOK OF WHOLESOME COUNSEL, translated from the Sanskrit by Francis Johnson; revised by Lionel D. Barnett; Chapman and Hall, London, 1923.

An easy-to-read translation, with footnotes surprisingly interesting even to the lay reader.

INDIAN FAIRY TALES, by Joseph Jacobs; Putnam, New York (no publication date given).

A splendid collection by the distinguished English folklorist of half a century ago.

JATAKAS, by E. B. Cowell; Cambridge University Press, Edinburgh and London, 1895.

This is the only comprehensive translation of the Jatakas in English, and many subsequent collections are based on this work or directly derived from it.

JATAKA TALES, edited by H. T. Francis and E. J. Thomas; Cambridge University Press, Edinburgh and London, 1916.

This book contains 116 Jatakas taken from the Cowell translation, to which have been added a group of extraordinary photographic illustrations of ancient carvings representing some of the Jatakas.

JATAKA TALES OF OLD INDIA, by Marguerite Aspinwall; Dutton, New York, 1927.

Twenty-nine Jatakas taken from Francis and Thomas and simplified for very young readers.

THE PANCHATANTRA, by Arthur W. Ryder; University of Chicago Press, Chicago, 1925.

A translation from the Sanskrit based on the text of Dr. J. Hertel, the German Orientalist who made an exhaustive study of the history and development of the Panchatantra.

THE PANCHATANTRA RECONSTRUCTED, by Franklin Edgerton; Vol. III in the American Oriental Series, Harvard University Press, Cambridge, Mass., 1923.

This literal translation of the Panchatantra is primarily for the scholar, but the introduction may interest the general reader.

A SHORT HISTORY OF INDIAN LITERATURE, by E. Horrwitz; T. Fisher Unwin, London, 1907.

This book contains a chapter on Hindu fables and presents a dozen proverbs and sayings from the Hitopadesa as rendered into English by Sir Monier Monier-Williams and Sir Edwin Arnold.

Acknowledgments

The work of the many scholars who, in the past century, have opened to the Western World India's great literary treasury was invaluable to me in the preparation of this book. I am particularly indebted to Franklin Edgerton, Arthur W. Ryder, B. Hale-Wortham, Sir Edwin Arnold, Francis Johnson, E. B. Cowell, T. W. Rhys Davids, H. T. Francis and E. J. Thomas.

To Professor Wyland D. Hand, folklorist at the University of California in Los Angeles; Dr. Judith M. Tyberg, director of the East-West Cultural Center of Los Angeles; Mary Margaret Dyer, head of work with children, Santa Monica Library; Dorothy Hansen, Chief, Children's Division, Los Angeles Public Library; Alice Stjernquist, Children's Librarian, Los Angeles County Public Library; Mrs. Paul H. Sheats of Westwood, California; and Swami Aseshananda of the Ramakrishna Monastery, California, I wish to express my thanks for reading this book in manuscript and for their valuable suggestions.

J.G.